Managers and Mandarins in Contemporary China

Are business conflicts in China resolved in much the same way as elsewhere? Or are they handled altogether differently? Setting out in search of an answer, Jie Tang immersed herself in the day-to-day operation of a major construction project in China that brought together participants from around the globe.

The result is this in-depth account of the inner workings of the Chinese business world. It follows the progress of construction from tendering to completion in an attempt to understand the progress and problems of the project as seen through the eyes of the participants. It also delves into how conflicts grew out of the structure of the project, as well as the broader context in which it operated. In doing so, *Managers and Mandarins in Contemporary China* touches on such issues as differing international standards and management procedures; the peculiarities of Chinese red tape; tensions between contractors; paternalism and nepotism; the role of campaigns; and the limits on contract in contemporary China. The book traces the increasing involvement of local officials in the work of the project, examining the reasons for this and its consequences for management.

Of interest to scholars and managers alike, this study benefits from the unparalleled access the author was able to secure to all the parties involved, Chinese and Western, commercial and governmental. Working alongside managers as a participant observer, the author uses the fine detail characteristic of ethnography to convey a vivid impression of how they faced up to conflict, intrigue, danger and a race against time. The result is a unique insight into the lives of managers in China today and the forces with which they have to contend.

Jie Tang, a native of Shanghai, has worked as a manager in both China and England, and has taught Chinese management at the School of Oriental and African Studies in London. She is the co-author of *The Changing Face of Chinese Management* (Routledge, 2003) and is currently developing international programmes for London University.

Routledge studies on the Chinese economy

Series Editor
Peter Nolan, University of Cambridge

Founding Series Editors
Peter Nolan, University of Cambridge
Dong Fureng, Beijing University

The aim of this series is to publish original, high-quality, research-level work by both new and established scholars in the West and the East, on all aspects of the Chinese economy, including studies of business and economic history.

Managers and Mandarins in Contemporary China
The building of an international business alliance

Jie Tang

Routledge
Taylor & Francis Group

LONDON AND NEW YORK

First published 2005
by Routledge
2 Park Square, Milton Park, Abingdon, Oxon OX14 4RN

Simultaneously published in the USA and Canada
by Routledge
270 Madison Ave, New York, NY 10016

Routledge is an imprint of the Taylor & Francis Group

© 2005 Jie Tang

Typeset in Times by
Florence Production Ltd, Stoodleigh, Devon
Printed and bound in Great Britain by
Antony Rowe Ltd, Chippenham, Wiltshire

British Library Cataloguing in Publication Data
A catalogue record for this book is available
from the British Library

Library of Congress Cataloging in Publication Data
A catalog record for this book has been requested

ISBN 0–415–36363–2 (hbk)

Contents

Illustrations

Figures

Table

Preface

This book attempts to understand how conflicts between the various parties involved in an international construction project in China were handled. It reflects my broader interest in the Chinese business world: in how it differs from elsewhere and in how it is changing. In a previous book, *The Changing Face of Chinese Management,* I looked at this on the basis of a series of interviews conducted with Chinese managers and officials drawn from across a broad spectrum of commercial activities. Here I focus on one particular case study, following the progress of a project as it unfolds from the vantage point of a participant observer.

One benefit is that it provides the inside knowledge necessary to correct the temptation to dismiss business practices that differ from one's own as stemming from ignorance of the proper way of doing things. This is flattering to one's self-esteem, but can simply reflect ignorance of what is at work. Better to follow Goffman's advice that 'any group of persons – prisoners, primitives, pilots or patients – develop a life of their own that becomes meaningful, reasonable and normal once you get close to it, and . . . a good way to learn about any of these worlds is to submit oneself in the company of the members to the daily round of petty contingencies to which they are subject' (1961: ix–x). This applies equally to the world of the Chinese manager, as we shall see.

Getting to grips with the practical difficulties of conducting such research in China throws an interesting light on the context in which management operates. I discuss this in Chapter 1. Chapter 2 sets the scene by outlining the nature of conflict management in China and in the construction industry. The story of what occurred on the project is then unfolded in Part II of the book, and those eager to cut to the chase may wish to start here, returning to the more general issues addressed in Part I later. I was fortunate in finding myself recording the history of a case that promised to have all the makings of a good story. The presence of dramatic interest was perhaps to be expected, given my focus on conflict, always a good ingredient in any tale. But I also found the project blessed with a cast of idiosyncratic characters, tensions, danger, intrigue and a race against time. In recounting how conflicts evolved and were handled on the project, I intertwine analysis with description throughout, though the balance between the two shifts somewhat as the story unfolds. Description dominates in the beginning, as the participants are introduced. I also present a more detailed account of the course of events in the early stages of the project in order to convey a more vivid impression of life on the project. Part III brings the story of the project after my departure up to date and reflects on the lessons to be learned.

My thanks to all those involved in the project for putting up with my presence so good-naturedly. Special gratitude is also due to Peter Nolan for all his encouragement and advice. Last, but not least, go thanks to Anthony Ward, my husband, for nagging me into keeping my field notes up to date when many a hard day's work on the site inclined me to put it off, and for being the source of endless insights into the perils and delights of cross-cultural partnership.

Part I

1 Introduction

This book grew out of a question that is easily posed: does the way Chinese managers handle conflict differ fundamentally from elsewhere or is it much the same? Finding the answer proves not quite so simple. At present, we just do not know enough about how conflict is managed within business in China. Even evidence from the West, where research on such matters is more plentiful, is far from adequate for purposes of comparison. Given such a starting point the present work does not pretend to offer a complete answer. Nevertheless, it does aim to throw fresh light on the problem, and a particularly intense light at that.

There are a number of ways one might set about finding answers to whether Chinese management has its own approach to conflict. One might compare the operation of Chinese companies with the operation of firms elsewhere in the world. Alternatively, one might study a situation where managers from China and overseas work together. This is the path I chose to follow. It led to my involvement in an international construction project in China, following its progress over the course of a year through an in-depth study based on participant observation.

Concentrating so intensively on one case yields rich results, but is not without its dangers. From a purely practical point of view, finding oneself with all one's eggs in one basket can at times be alarming. This I found at the very outset, when the first lesson I learned about the behaviour of multinational companies is that information fed in on one side of the globe may well not end up where it was hoped on the other. I had approached the London office of Moreland,* an international project management company, seeking permission to observe one of its construction projects in China. The human resources director was sympathetic, but as China came under the authority of another region administered from Australia, he promised to forward my request to his counterpart there, adding his

---

* A list of the organizations and individuals involved in my research can be found in the Appendix. Their names have been changed throughout this account in order to preserve anonymity.

recommendation. Despite waiting several weeks, no reply came, and I eventually set out for China still without a project to study. Given my intention of undertaking a detailed study of one case, this caused me no little degree of nervousness. Barley's description of how his anthropological fieldtrip to Africa to study a particular ceremony came to nothing when a plague of caterpillars infesting the local crops was taken as a bad omen and led to the ritual being called off, came to mind (Barley 1987). In my case, the local fauna were unlikely to prove a problem (although, as we shall see, a dog was to feature), but was I nonetheless to travel all the way to China only to find myself with no project to study?

Initial enquiries on arrival only served to increase my anxiety. Unable to make contact with Moreland on arrival, I asked around among managers known to me who were working for Chinese state-owned enterprises engaged in construction. One was involved in negotiating with several foreign companies. Could I observe the negotiations or the operation of the subsequent project? 'Impossible,' came the reply. The negotiations were secret and no state enterprise would allow an independent scholar to observe their workings at close hand. Suitably downhearted I eventually made contact with the manager at Moreland to whom I needed to speak. He had not had my proposal passed on to him by the Australia office, but was prepared to see me. I went along and explained my interest in studying an international construction project at first hand, and my background in the industry. To my relief, he showed no surprise at what I had in mind and, subject to checking my bona fides with my Moreland contact in London and with Cambridge, he was happy to let me start on the site the following Monday. I was greatly relieved. The project was just what I was looking for. It was in construction, an area with which I was familiar, it brought together partners from diverse national backgrounds, and tendering had just commenced. I was to be on the site from Monday to Thursday from nine to five every week, leaving Fridays free to conduct further research offsite. In the event, I was also to find myself attending the site on Fridays and at weekends when important meetings were scheduled. The observation went on to span eleven months, from August 2000 to July 2001, supplemented by three follow-up visits.

The different reception from Moreland and Chinese state enterprises to the notion of allowing outside observers to monitor projects is instructive and reflects differing attitudes to transparency and experience with independent research. The manager I had originally approached at Moreland in London was at ease with the idea, mentioning how there were already two PhD students studying project management on Moreland's sites in the UK. Similarly, their project manager in China found the prospect of the project being studied perfectly natural and unobjectionable. For Chinese managers in state enterprises, however, the notion was new and suspect. Study by a current employee might be possible, but not by someone turning up from outside except in the unlikely event of being imposed from above.

A number of influences appear to be at work here. First, there is the greater suspicion of outsiders one would expect of the more collectivist outlook prevailing in China in comparison with many Western countries. The cultural climate will shape the ease with which certain methods can be employed. Politically and, given the dominance of the state in industry, economically, China is a far less open society than many in the West. Journalists from Hong Kong have found themselves facing espionage charges for publishing details of state enterprises that elsewhere would be regarded as uncontroversial and as lying within the public domain. At the level of the workplace, sensitivity by insiders to what they perceive as criticism by an outsider means the observer has to exercise considerable tact to avoid causing offence.

Observation of a local court, undertaken during my fieldwork to provide me with background material on dispute resolution, provided further illustration of the official attitude towards openness. According to government announcements, any citizen is entitled to attend court other than in cases involving state secrets or certain matters bearing on individual privacy. Nonetheless, I took the precaution of securing through family friends an invitation to meet with one of the judges. Connections in China, direct or through family and friends, play a large part in facilitating access that is otherwise routinely denied. On arrival, a bailiff asked me where I was going. When I replied that I was going to attend court, he told me there were guards stationed outside each courtroom to stop people getting in. What about the right to attend, I asked. 'It's no good telling them that', he told me. 'They earn 600 yuan [about £48] a month, they don't know what the law is, all they know is to stop people getting in.' Fortunately, there was my contact to fall back on and I was finally able to gain entry.

To a lack of familiarity with independent academic research, a suspicion of outsiders and a general lack of openness may be added fears related to the uncovering of hidden interests. As we shall see, there was a widespread caution among Chinese staff on the project against saying or doing anything that might unwittingly impinge upon the hidden interests and intrigues of others, especially those of their superiors. Such an atmosphere is hardly conducive to welcoming the prying eye of an inquisitive outsider.

Trust, suspicion and the importance of being earnest

The barriers to trust just touched upon did not evaporate on entry to the project. Rifts between the various parties involved further complicated the situation. Prominent among these were tensions between the joint venture partners commissioning the project. These were a consortium of German exhibition firms and a Chinese state-owned land development corporation. Wariness on both sides had led to the establishment of a project management team internally divided along parallel lines, with Moreland being nominated by the German side to safeguard its interests.

The Chinese partners nominated their own members of the project management team. Entering into the project under the aegis of Moreland thus entailed an initial identification with one side that aroused suspicion about my role on the part of some, at least, of the other.

Fortunately, I eventually overcame this in most cases, although not all. Where suspicion persisted, the barriers it presented were often overcome by having established rapport with other members of the project. I was excluded, for example, from certain meetings held exclusively for the Chinese staff of the joint venture. The first time I encountered this the Chinese staff returning from the meeting said that they had been instructed not to talk about what had transpired, although gossip was to ensure that I was soon to hear. Subsequently such meetings took place after rapport had been established with those called upon to attend and information flowed more freely. Chinese staff sharing my office returned from one such meeting that had evidently been intended to inspire ideological commitment to meeting project targets. 'Tang Jie, you should have been there to see what the real management style in China is like. It was just like going back to the Cultural Revolution,' said one, before everyone went on to recall the tone and message of the meeting, telling me to 'write it down in your book.'

Indeed, a number of the staff with whom I established close relationships took an increasingly active interest in my work as we got to know one another, and proved most helpful in making notes for me of meetings that took place while I was elsewhere. This was partly a matter of establishing good relations, partly a matter of proving my serious intent. Although frequent comments could be heard poking fun at those who put their heart and soul into their work, at a deeper level those who displayed competence and diligence attracted respect. There was initially an expectation among some of the staff that I might be there purely as a matter of form, with whatever observation I had in mind being superficial at best. However, my regular hours of work and odd appetite for attending endless meetings, soon disabused them of this notion. Similarly, going out to tour the construction site was viewed by those members of the project team who preferred to manage at arms length and not to stray from the office more than was necessary as going beyond the call of duty. My talking to the ordinary workers, however, was viewed by many of the staff with a certain amount of bemusement. Direct conversation with workers was rare even among members of the project management team who did venture out onto the site. For all its communist ideology, China remains deeply hierarchical in outlook, and construction workers are commonly looked down upon as of little worth or understanding. Furthermore, it quite simply meant getting mud on one's boots, something not to the taste of the aspiring mandarin. As we shall see later, there was a preoccupation with preserving the 'civilized' status of the site, one which often boiled down to a pressing concern that visiting dignitaries would have properly paved and swept surfaces to drive over and to walk upon.

With time, I was also able to extend the boundaries of trust. Later in the project I was to attend many meetings held by the general contractor and came to be regarded as an insider in front of whom sensitive information that was not for general consumption could be discussed. Speaking of a letter from the project management that construction should cease on a certain part of the building until a problem had been redressed, the chair of the meeting remarked: 'I can say this because Ms Tang is one of us, we do not need to pay any attention to these letters.'

Attempts to include me within one circle or another did at times pose a dilemma. I was frequently asked to assist as an interpreter, a role I welcomed as offering some repayment for the hospitality extended to me by the project and as an opportunity to be better integrated into the work of the organization. The language divide when the different nationalities met was, methodologically, most helpful, as it often meant that comments that in other meetings would be made behind the scenes and thus might escape observation, were made there and then, sometimes with the injunction: 'Don't translate this.'

My policy here was to comply, but to preserve my neutrality, to explain my silence by passing on my instructions to the foreign manager. In all cases but one, they understood, finding the situation wryly amusing. However, a newly arrived American member of the project management team took offence and wrote to the owners complaining that the 'interpreter' had been told to stop translating at one point. Fortunately, the matter blew over, as more important problems were by then plaguing the project.

In many ways, my peculiar position made it impossible for me to act as many interpreters, who are expected by the side employing them to edit what is being said to advance the interests of one side over the other. The demands of my other role as an observer struggling to maintain her independence made this impossible in my case. This often led to frustration on the part of the Chinese participants. On one occasion, I translated an instruction given in English by the German owner that construction should be halted so that a structural fault could be addressed. This was in the presence of government officials. The Chinese manager from the general contractor, who does not speak English, immediately announced to the meeting that I had misunderstood and that the German manager had not said anything of the kind. However, my neutrality did have unexpected benefits. It was to lead to me being invited to attend meetings where important business decisions had to be made on the basis that I could be relied upon by all sides to get matters straight, however annoying this might prove on other occasions.

One cannot participate over an extended period without taking part in the give-and-take of information and gossip; an observer who silently observed without contributing to the ongoing stream of discussion would be the opposite of unobtrusive. This is particularly pertinent in a collectivist culture. Chinese managers are more suspicious than many of their Western counterparts when it comes to answering questions from an outsider. One way to break the ice is to prompt them by indicating that you have talked with their boss and colleagues. They then feel safer and more relaxed and talk without inhibition. This must be balanced, of course, with preserving confidences. I generally succeeded in this difficult balancing act, but on one occasion I inadvertently threw one Chinese manager into a fury with his junior managers when I mentioned an agreement I had seen them reach of which they had failed to inform him.

Apart from odd instances such as that, my presence as an outside observer did not seem to disturb the natural course of events. Partly this was because I was just one among many. People may have adjusted their behaviour when addressing me directly, but in general, their attention was fixed elsewhere, on their colleagues or the problem at hand. My presence on the project was soon accepted as everyday by the Chinese staff with whom I shared an office. I was soon regarded as an insider, a not entirely unmixed blessing as my taste in clothes and more or less everything else became the target of frank and forthright attempts to bring me into line with group norms and sensibilities. I was even cajoled into joining karaoke outings, the ultimate test of an ethnographer's dedication.

Location

Few things in planning an ethnography of management behaviour can be as important as the location of one's desk. Nonetheless, where I was going to be located was not something to which I had given much thought. In the event, I ended up by pure good fortune in the best possible spot. It seemed at first I might end up sharing an office with the general manager of the joint venture commissioning the project. This may appear to the uninitiated as the best possible location, right at the hub of the enterprise. In fact the general manager, a German, was largely marginalized, an isolated figure on the borders of the day-to-day work of the construction project. I finished up instead in the commercial department of the project management team. This was relatively low in hierarchical terms, but proved an ideal location for gathering information. It played a vital part in the tendering process and was later the point of contact for contractors pressing for payment and special consideration. All matters revolving around costs found their way there. It was also the focal point for unofficial social gatherings and the exchange of gossip. This was partly attributable to it being staffed entirely by young unmarried women, partly to a cupboard kept well stocked on diverted company expenses with a changing variety of fruit and snacks. Given the combination of a mainly male staff and a culture fascinated by food in which socializing revolves around eating, the combination proved an irresistible attraction.

The benefits of my strategic location were not lost upon others. The head of the Chinese half of the project management team, who was clearly suspicious of my presence, suggested that I should move to another office that just happened to be much more of a quiet backwater, on the grounds that the office I was sharing was 'too crowded'. This was universally understood by those sharing the office as a politely veiled order, but I stuck my heels in and, treating the invitation at its face value, politely declined. This caused much surprise and amusement among my new found colleagues and was taken as a sign of how hopelessly Westernized I had become. Nonetheless, it worked, and I remained.

Lunchtime in the canteen also proved a valuable spot to both gather and disseminate information. My purpose on the site had not been generally announced on my arrival, though I was able to clarify this to everyone by simply replying to a fellow diner's enquiries shortly after my arrival. Everyone could be overheard and everyone clearly had ears pinned for picking up information, myself included. I learned to cultivate the habit of eating slowly and returning again and again to the soup tureen to replenish my bowl to justify lingering over my lunch. This required some courage. Free soup is a feature of state unit canteens, and young people saving for their wedding or older people saving for their children's weddings will fight for the soup to avoid having to buy dishes. These people are disparagingly referred to as '*tang bao* – soup dumplings', an epithet I could see myself as being well on the way to acquiring. Another interpretation of my lingering over lunch came from a senior manager. Reaching back into her memory for what she had been taught of English table manners, which she evidently assumed I had picked up while living in England, she sought to reassure me. 'It's all right to leave the table, you know,' she kindly counselled. 'You don't to wait until everyone else has finished.'

Taking an ethnographic approach to the study of management has the advantage over interviews of being able to observe people in locations away from the more formal environment of the office. Jamming into overcrowded taxis after work inspires a certain camaraderie, especially when conspiring to duck down surplus passengers to avoid the gaze of passing traffic police. Matters such as attitudes towards the Communist Party are more freely discussed in the safer atmosphere of a shuttle bus than at work. Similarly, responses to the conflicts at work tended to differ with setting. As people fell back into their seats for the journey home they would often shift into taking a more even-handed approach to problems and their own part in them than in the more fraught atmosphere of work.

Sources and interpretation

An intensive case study also offers the advantage of ready access to a variety of sources that can be called upon to fill in gaps in one's knowledge, to confirm reports and to reveal inconsistencies. As explained earlier, my presence on the project was as a participant observer, assisting with translation work. This meant that many documents such as contracts and meeting minutes passed through my hands. In addition, I was given free access to the project management files. These revealed conflicts left unvoiced, at least in my presence. A report might convey, as in the case of one example, a complaint to the owner by a Chinese manager against a visiting representative of the German side infringing on his authority and calling for this to be stopped. Not only did such files serve to fill in gaps in my knowledge, they were also able on occasion to serve to settle points of uncertainty. I was told by some of the staff, for example, that one Chinese manager who had a more than usually authoritarian approach had served as a guard on the Chinese equivalent of the Gulag. Another, however, told me that they were just pulling my leg. I was a little surprised at this, as such teasing is rare as a form of workplace humour in this part of China, certainly far less common than it seems in Britain. The matter was finally settled in favour of the original story when I stumbled across a CV of the manager in a contract application I had been given to check.

Such straightforward confirmation and filling in of missing links is naturally satisfying, but at times difficult to secure. At times one finds oneself with loose ends and little more than hunches to go on. At other times, one does not lack evidence, but the evidence is contradictory and the problem becomes how to interpret this. Take, for example, the situation in which one party to the construction project that has been antagonistic to another does an about-face literally overnight. This was a common occurrence. Those working on the project who were not directly involved would routinely attribute such a change to the newly compliant party having been visited the night before by the other side and persuaded by one means or another to adopt a more conciliatory approach. The delicacy of this matter made it difficult to substantiate such claims by straightforward enquiry, but in one particular case I was able to establish that this was exactly what had happened. Given this evidence and that such practices are mentioned as commonplace in China in conversations with managers and that the participants on the project had sufficiently long experience of their trade to know what they are talking about, the suggestion must be that similar visits probably lay behind many another overnight change of heart.

This strikes me as interesting and suggestive, but not, of course, conclusive, except in the one case that I was able to substantiate. Even in the seemingly unlikely event, however, that those involved in the project were in every other case wrong in their explanation of such events, their belief that this is what lay behind them is interesting in itself. A long-established sociological maxim holds that if people believe something to be true, then it is true in its consequences. In other words, if people believe that hidden understandings arrived at outside the office pervade the operation of the project, their behaviour will change in consequence. This, as we shall see, turns out to be the case.

Problems of interpretation also surround those who display considerable variation in the opinions they express. It is a matter of everyday experience that some characters are more transparent than others, tending to do what they say and to say what they mean. These pose no problem. Those who say one thing and do another, or whose opinions change from one setting to the next, are more puzzling. This is as true for their colleagues as it was for me. Key players in the project ran between those generally recognized by all concerned as fairly transparent in terms of their concerns and outlook to those whose position and interests were regarded as difficult to discern and whose likely response was consequently difficult to predict. This is doubtless largely a matter of personality. Nevertheless, it is interesting to note that the fault line that ran throughout the project between the Chinese and foreign sides left all those key players widely perceived as one-dimensional standing on one side of the divide and all the characters more generally accepted as impenetrably complex on the other. This, of course, may have been pure coincidence, but the evidence suggests that these apparent quirks of character flourish in certain social climates.

The attitudes that people have are often ambivalent and the values they entertain in conflict with each other. Observation over an extended period and in a variety of settings can give greater insight into such internal conflicts, which often echo external ones. In some cases, conduct would seem at odds with conviction. In casual conversation, for example, many managers would ridicule the various campaigns launched to breathe enthusiasm into their efforts on the project. This did not mean, however, that they paid them little heed. On the contrary, other sources confirmed that these same managers were very active in their efforts to secure the various honorific awards on offer and to make speeches at the campaign meetings, a point to which we shall return. Ever eager to cross-check sources, I teased one or two of these managers with whom I was on particularly friendly terms with the news that I had heard they were eager to make speeches at the rallies, at which they looked suitably sheepish.

Opposing interests ever accompany a disposition to be economical with the truth. In such a situation, the ethnographer is not alone in puzzling over what others are attempting. Speaking, for example, to one of the German directors involved in the original negotiations to establish the joint venture, he interpreted what he saw as willingness by the Chinese side to make concessions on minor points in the negotiations as deriving from a cultural concern with maintaining harmony. Speaking to negotiators on the Chinese side, however, a very different picture emerged. What had been taken as minor concessions were remembered with bitterness as major ones that were only made as the team was under political instructions to secure the contract and could not afford to let the negotiations break down. Any attachment to maintaining harmony as an end in itself was far from their minds, though such sentiments may well have been conveyed in an attempt to avoid tipping their hand.

Comparison and exasperation

Looking at one project intensively over an extended period of time yielded much that could never have been gathered by other techniques such as interviews. It poses the question, however, about whether the project was representative. Does it serve as a basis on which broader conclusions can be based?

From the point of view of one tradition often associated with ethnography, the question might seem misplaced. For social anthropologists such as Leach, the tools of their trade are not aimed at putting hypotheses to the test, but at interpreting meaning and promoting understanding. As he remarks:

> The fundamental characteristic of human culture is its endless diversity. . . . Anthropologists who imagine . . . they can reduce the observations of ethnographers to a nomothetic natural science are wasting their time. Anthropology is not, and should not aim to be, a 'science' in the natural science sense. If anything it is a form of art. In any genuine science the only assertions which are of interest are potentially open to refutation. Most of the propositions put forward by social anthropologists . . . are not of this refutable kind. When they are they are immediately refuted . . .
>
> (Leach 1982: 51–2)

There is much in my work that sits at ease with this perspective, trying as I was to understand events through unravelling the often contrary interpretations of those involved.

Similarly, much that appeared unreasonable at the start of my fieldwork became less so as it progressed, which is part of what attracted me to an ethnographic approach. Take meetings, for example. From the perspective of Western management principles, most appeared to plumb the depths of irrationality in the chaotic manner in which they were conducted. For some outsiders, there is the temptation to attribute the difference to ignorance, or, more kindly, lack of training. Indeed, having honed my own managerial skills within Western companies, this was not far off my own initial exasperated reaction.

However, exasperated reactions are always worth paying attention to. They usually indicate that there is something you have failed to appreciate. In her ethnography of the Shanghai Stock Exchange, for example, Hertz comments that few things irritated her as much as the answer she received when she asked people why they invested on the Stock Exchange. 'Because we are poor,' was the invariable reply (Hertz 1998: 8). At first, she simply ignored it, or set about stubbornly explaining to the richer ones that this could not be so. It took time (and a blazing row with one of her Chinese friends) before she began to appreciate that what was being said was coloured by the notions her respondents had of themselves as Chinese in relation to their Western interviewer.

Similarly with Roy's pioneering ethnography of the workplace, what seemed at first the irritatingly senseless 'jabbering' of his new found work-mates came to take on meaning; with increasing familiarity 'the nonsense made sense, the obscure became clear, and the silly actually funny' (Roy 1960: 158). What is needed, then, is time, time to become accustomed to a different world with its own assumptions rather than prematurely attempting to assimilate them to one's own. In my own case, it was only through participating in meetings over a long period that I was able to appreciate that participants were able to move back and forth between formality and apparent chaos, casting doubt on my initial idea that the apparent disorder was due to lack of training in the proper way of conducting business.

Some ethnographers, as I have mentioned, are wary of comparison. Even for those who favour it, there are constraints. Everything has the defects of its qualities: while the time taken up by ethnography ensures depth, it leaves little over for gathering comparative data by direct observation of other cases. In addition, I know of no other case study similar enough to my own on which secondary analysis might be based. I was, however, fortunate in having another avenue open to me. The project brought together managers with a wealth of experience of working on similar projects within China and elsewhere. They were to turn out to be my pool of research associates, as I frequently turned to them to elicit valuable insights into the similarities and differences between this project and others. In addition, I was able to draw upon my own experience of working in joint ventures within the construction industry in China.

Data gathering and analysis

The actual details of gathering data involved a mixture of hard work and a tough hide. As mentioned earlier, the data were principally gathered over an eleven-month period. Being on the other side of town from where I was living, this entailed working nine to five on most days plus three hours travel. At the end of each tiring day, I had to discipline myself to type up my field notes based on conversations and observations at work. To aid my memory I jotted down notes on the spot. (I went equipped with a tape recorder, but in the event, I judged this too intrusive to use.)

A thick skin was needed in a male-dominated world where some managers were quick to take the opportunity to flatter themselves at my expense. It was here, however, that my note-taking came to my defence. I wrote all my notes in English, partly for confidentiality, partly because this was how they were to be typed up. This was so even when I was conducting or listening to conversations in Chinese. Owing to the prestige surrounding writing in China the fact that I could transcribe Chinese conversation simultaneously in English aroused considerable awe among managers who had previously been dismissive, and they would proudly point out what I was doing to newcomers as evidence they were being studied by, in their own words, a female prodigy.

I observed an average of three meetings a day during my stay, amounting to over 600 in total. They included meetings between and within all the companies involved in the project at all levels. Examples include meetings between the general contractor and its subcontractors; between the architect and the contractors; between the project management and contractors; between the project management and the owner; and between the district or municipal government and the contractors. I was able to participate in most of the internal meetings held by any of these players on the site. Sometimes my presence gave surprise to the participants, inviting the inevitable comment: 'We have to come to this boring meeting, do you have to as well?' or jokes along the lines 'this is a secret meeting, you are not allowed.'

I was also given access to all written communications on the site. These included all of the contracts, progress reports, meeting minutes and site memos, and even extended to the occasional anonymous letter. Eventually the project manager from Moreland introduced me to newcomers as the 'most informed person on the site' and I was invited on this basis by the general manager of the joint venture to brief a new member of his management team on what was going on.

Apart from these official sources, I also observed most of the informal commercial negotiations and technical discussions taking place between the project management and the contractors. I also participated in many of the site inspections and tours taken by the project management, the architects and government officials.

In the days when I was not on the site, I paid visits to the headquarters of the companies involved in the project and interviewed their senior managers. This gave me a better understanding of the companies, and a fuller understanding of what lay behind the behaviour of their managers on the site. Interviews with retired senior managers in the companies turned out to be especially fruitful. They are retained as advisers by their companies, so they are well informed, have more time and are less restrained in making critical comments. In addition, I conducted interviews with competitors so that I could reach a better understanding of the general situation of the industries involved. At the same time, I also took the opportunity to conduct interviews with government officials, and state and private companies in other business lines to understand government industrial policy and the business environment in China.

I naturally approached the project with many ideas concerning what might prove to be at work in shaping how conflicts were managed from my reading of the literature on the topic and my previous experience in the field. Other ideas emerged in the course of my observation of the project, both at the time and subsequently through going through my notes with the aid of a program entitled Non-numerical Unstructured Data Indexing Searching and Theorizing, more fondly known as NUDIST. I approached the analysis at each stage with what I hope was an open mind, and certainly found that my ideas changed considerably in the course of my research. Some were abandoned, others refined, while altogether new connections came to light as I discovered more about the project and the day-to-day life of those involved in it.

2 Conflict, culture and construction

Before turning to events on the project, it will help in understanding the forces at work if we draw together some of what can be gleaned about management and conflict from other works. With this end in mind, the first section of this chapter outlines a general perspective on the place of conflict in organizational life. The second turns to consider what is distinctive about the Chinese way of handling of conflict. Having discussed a number of core traditional values, I move on in section three to consider how far these have been affected by the dramatic social and economic changes experienced by China in recent years.

Construction is an industry particularly prone to conflict. This has to be borne in mind to avoid attributing to cultural differences clashes that might occur in any event, given the nature of the industry. Hence the final section of the chapter gives a brief introduction to the organizational problems facing construction and the means that have been evolved to cope with them.

Conflict and management

My aim was to study how conflict was handled within an international venture. However, starting out on a study of a project in search of conflict might appear to pose a problem in terms of bias. Might there not be the risk of ending up with a distorted picture, seeing conflict and intrigue at every turn? Awareness of the possibility can itself serve as part of the solution. Another safeguard lies in taking a balanced approach to the role of conflict. Much analysis of organizations tends, following a broader split within the social sciences, to see them as primarily based either on consensus or on conflict (Burrell and Morgan 1979). My approach follows a somewhat different tradition, one that insists that the study of conflict is inextricably bound up with the study of cooperation, with social life being a shifting mix of the two. It provides a model of organizational life that fits well with the world of shifting alliances and subterranean interests in which I was to find myself.

The mention of conflict tends to conjure up an image of something that is episodic, a break in the natural course of events, a breach of the peace. It also evokes images of violent opponents, eyeball to eyeball, swapping blows. However, many studies of conflict embrace a far broader range of thought, feeling and behaviour. They start from the assumption that conflict is not episodic, but is part and parcel of every aspect of life. Relationships are not simply cooperative or antagonistic, but a blend of both. This reaches even into intimate relationships; perhaps, as the maxim maintains, in the misfortunes of our dearest friends there is something not entirely displeasing to us.

In addition to conflict and cooperation intermingling in one relationship, other ties link the two. As is commonly observed, conflict between groups fosters solidarity within them. Writing almost a century ago, Cooley used the business world by way of illustration:

> You can resolve the social order into a great number of co-operative wholes of various sorts, each of which includes conflicting elements within itself upon which it is imposing some sort of harmony with a view to conflict with other wholes. Thus the mind of man is full of wrangling impulses, but his struggle with the world requires he acts as a unit. A labor-union is made up of competing and disputing members, but they must manage to agree when it comes to a struggle with the employer. And employer and employees, whatever their struggles, must and do combine into a whole for the competition of their plant against others.
>
> (Cooley 1966: 39)

From this perspective, conflict pervades far more of organizational life than the occasional shouting match. The individuals or units in conflict may have different statuses (e.g. labour vs. management), different positions in the organization (e.g. headquarters vs. subsidiary) or may belong to different organizations (e.g. partners in joint ventures, customers and suppliers). When those involved belong to different cultures, as was often the case in the project studied here, mutual misunderstanding and distrust can easily compound matters.

Giving greater attention to conflict brings into focus aspects of organizational life otherwise overlooked. What might be dubbed organizational misbehaviour, for example, often remains peripheral to the study of organizational behaviour. However, far from being rare, such behaviour is routine. Employees are not, as some standard texts seem to imply, almost entirely conforming and dutiful. On the contrary, however regrettable it may seem, they frequently give way to doing things at work they are not supposed to do. Ackroyd and Thompson illustrate a broad range of such misconduct, ascribing it to employees 'recognizing that there is not a precise correspondence between their own interests and those of their employing company, and acting accordingly' (1999: 2).

A number of other traditions in the study of organizations have focused on just such a mismatch in interests and its consequences. Agency theory, for example, has focused on how principals face the need to curb opportunism on the part of their agents through adjusting rewards and information systems (Eisenhardt 1989). Transaction cost economics shares with agency theory the assumption that individuals may well give way to the temptation to pursue their self-interest with guile, distorting information and being economical with the truth (Williamson 1981).

Political models of organizations share this sensitivity to conflicts of interest within and between organizations. Power, the focus of their attention, rests on the effectiveness of channels of communication. This is why power is so bound up with administration, which is essentially the processing of information. When the channels fail to work effectively, whether through misunderstanding or the deliberate withholding of information by those lower in the hierarchy, control is weakened (Pettigrew 1973). Clashes of interest can also become entangled with barriers to horizontal communication that hinder overall effectiveness, as when one side in an alliance strives to keep commercial secrets from the other for fear of future competition. Principals struggling to control their agents and participants being more than economical with the truth were, as we shall see, to feature prominently to shaping the course of events on the project.

Insisting on attention to human frailties, to how things are rather than to how they ought to be, is a refreshing characteristic of such approaches. Yet conventional wisdom and perhaps the truth of the matter holds that frailty is not evenly distributed, else resources would not be devoted to detecting qualities of character when selecting agents. The belief is fondly held that trustworthiness is not merely a quality of circumstance, but of moral fibre. Trustworthiness, nonetheless, is not solely a question of character. Where the boundaries of trust are drawn differs from one social milieu to another, a point to which we shall return.

Conflict has been described as beginning 'when one party perceives that the other has negatively affected, or is about to negatively affect, something that he or she cares about' (Thomas 1992: 653). This may well be where it begins. Whether or not it is given voice, however, is another matter, for where there is an imbalance of power it may seem as well at times to hold one's tongue. The conflict itself may remain latent, with one side deliberately kept in the dark about damage dealt to its interests. Dawson has drawn out the possibilities, as summarized in Table 2.1.

Once it emerges, conflict can be approached in a variety of different ways. Using an approach developed by Thomas, we can distinguish the five orientations charted in Figure 2.1. The first dimension, shown on the vertical axis, measures the desire to satisfy one's own concerns, varying in strength from unassertive to assertive. The second, shown on the horizontal axis, measures one's desire to satisfy the concerns of the other party, varying from uncooperative to cooperative. Taken together, the two dimensions present five ways of handling conflict. The competitive approach reflects

Table 2.1 Overt and covert conflict

Expression of conflict	Knowledge about issue over which there is conflict between interested parties	Action of interested parties to press own interest
Overt	Known to all parties	All parties press own interest
Degrees of covertness	Known to all parties	Some parties do not press own interest because they consider they will be unsuccessful, or otherwise fear consequences
	Known to all parties	Some parties do not press own interest because they consider the dominance of another partner is legitimate
	Known to some parties but not to others	Some parties excluded from pressing own interest
	Not seen as an issue, part of taken-for-granted world	No specific action

Source: from Dawson (1996: 171)

a desire to have one's own way regardless of anyone else. In contrast, the accommodative approach is one of appeasement, of self-sacrifice for the sake of the relationship. Intermediate between these two attitudes we find sharing, a taste for 'splitting the difference' in which both parties compromise to gain a degree of satisfaction, albeit incomplete. The collaborative approach seeks to integrate the concerns of both parties, aiming at fully satisfying both through devising a mutually beneficial solution. The avoidant approach favours benign neglect.

Such distinctions are not new to management theory. As early as 1925 Follett was discussing the differences between domination, compromise and integration as means of dealing with conflict, equivalent to Thomas's competitive, sharing and collaborative modes. Follett was active in promoting integration as a means of harnessing conflict constructively, while realizing that it was not as widespread as might be hoped (Graham 1995). As Child remarks in discussing Follett's work in relation to his own on joint ventures in Hungary and China: 'Integration was the declared aspiration of a number of foreign joint venture partners, but was actually found in only a few cases' (Child 1995: 94). More common was domination in the form of forced learning or passive imitation or compromise by segmenting the operation into separate zones of influence for each partner.

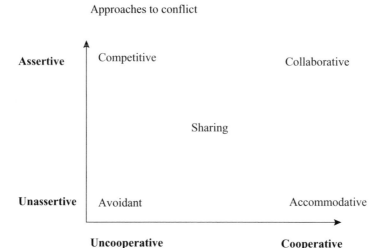

Figure 2.1 Conflict orientations
Source: adapted from Thomas (1992: 668)

Which of the five approaches outlined in Figure 2.1 is favoured appears to depend in part on the cultural background of those involved. This can be seen in a comparison of Chinese and British attitudes to conflict resolution undertaken by Tang and Kirkbride (1986). Using a questionnaire designed to measure which of the five solutions identified by Thomas was most preferred they compared two groups of British and Chinese Hong Kong government officials with similar rank and background. A third group of Chinese managers from the private sector was also included. The Chinese managers, both public and private, favoured solutions revolving around compromise and avoidance in contrast with the British officials, who preferred reliance on competition and collaboration. A number of other cross-cultural studies lend support to this image of a Chinese cultural preference for compromise. Leung (1987), for example, found Chinese subjects in Hong Kong favouring mediation over adjudication as a means of settling disputes, in contrast with a comparable group of Americans, who had no preference for one over the other.

Cultural considerations enter into the equation when selecting conflict strategies in more ways than simply shaping general preferences. The distance between those in dispute will also play a part. Members of the 'ingroup', those with whom one feels a shared sense of affinity, may well be tackled differently from those seen as belonging to the 'outgroup'. As one summary of research on this topic reports: 'Outgroup members are believed to be less attractive, less capable, less trustworthy, less honest, less co-operative, and less deserving than members of the ingroup' (Weldon and Jehn 1996: 98). Such beliefs can easily lead to the use of different strategies for insiders and outsiders. This is particularly likely in collectivist cultures, where we can expect a sharp difference in the behaviour of individuals according to whether they are interacting with 'ingroup' or 'outgroup' members.

Chinese attitudes to conflict

It is sometimes difficult for those living in individualist cultures to appreciate that the values related to the individual they cherish are far from universal. More people in the world live in collectivist societies that take a different stance on individual rights and duties. Such societies are characterized by intense social interaction within relatively closed groups, leading to a corresponding stress on the need to maintain harmony. Open confrontation is deemed rude and flat refusal replaced by delay or a 'yes' that everyone understands should not be taken literally. Individualist cultures are uneasy with such behaviour rather than applauding it as good manners. Good character is seen to reside in plain-speaking. A child who always reflects the opinions of others is regarded as a weak character. To the collectivist, in contrast, the child who continually disagrees with others is the one at fault.

The collectivist approach to life draws a sharp distinction between those who belong and those who do not, between us and them, the former trusted, the latter suspect. This clearly has important implications for business. Enterprises are seen as ideally based on moral ties reminiscent of the family rather than cold contract. Favouring insiders is more to be expected than frowned upon. This contrasts with the universalism of individualistic cultures with their suspicion of nepotism. For the collectivist, entering into a serious business relationship with an outsider requires time spent on establishing trust, the task has to wait upon the relationship. Only then can business be addressed, with trust serving in place of contracts that cover every detail.

The division between collectivist and individualist societies is related to another that revolves around attitudes to power and authority. This concerns the extent to which the less powerful members of institutions and organizations expect and accept that power will be distributed unequally. In societies that place a high value on respect for authority those wielding power can rely on deference from those below, with subordinates expecting to be told what to do rather than to be consulted. In such societies authority figures can expect to be accorded respect and will not be amused if it is not forthcoming.

Such attitudes towards authority can be entrenched early in life. In high-deference societies parents teach their children obedience and expect to be treated with respect. In contrast, parents and children in low-deference societies are more inclined to treat each other as equals. Similar differences prevail between teachers and students, while later in life the ideal boss for those valuing deference is the benevolent autocrat, for those of the opposite persuasion the resourceful democrat (Hofstede 1994: 37). In deferential societies people take with them into adulthood not merely the habit of outward respect for seniors, but also comfort from depending upon them. There is the assumption that this is a quite natural desire. In low-deference societies humans are viewed in a reverse fashion, as impelled to struggle to break free from dependence.

Both collectivism and deference to authority have been central to life in China for so many centuries that the pursuit of 'harmony-in-hierarchy' has been suggested as the key to understanding much of Chinese social behaviour (Bond and Hwang 1986: 213–14). It is an ideal that many trace back deep into Chinese antiquity, attributing its influence to the teachings of Confucius and his fundamental concern with maintaining social harmony.

This philosophy departs from the Western tendency to make the isolated individual as its starting point. For from the Confucian perspective, the idea of the isolated individual appears as an unnatural and absurd abstraction. Instead, we are viewed as inseparable from our relationships with others. Fulfilment is to be found in the performance of one's social roles and obligations rather than in breaking free of them. Our key relationships are viewed in hierarchical terms, with the senior party granted authority over the junior. Such rights, however, are balanced by rules of correct behaviour (*li*). Those exercising authority are expected to do so with benevolence and justice.

Evidence of an enduring faith in harmony-in-hierarchy among the Chinese can be found in a number of contemporary cross-cultural comparisons of values. Prominent among these has been the work of Hofstede (1980). This grew out of a comparison of the work values of IBM employees spread throughout more than fifty countries. On two of the value dimensions to emerge from Hofstede's study, Hong Kong, Singapore and Taiwan share a similar profile, being low in individualism and high in terms of deference to those in authority. When applied to mainland China, Hofstede's questionnaire yielded similar results (Bond and Hwang 1986: 228). This particular configuration of values is not unique to Chinese societies, however, but is shared by others such as Greece, Iran, Turkey, Pakistan, Thailand, India and the Philippines. It is a pattern that does, nonetheless, stand Chinese societies in opposition to many Western countries. These include countries such as the United States, Britain and Germany, which score relatively high on Hofstede's individualism index and low on his measure of deference. With managers and professionals of all three nationalities participating in the project, a clash of outlook with Chinese colleagues appeared a distinct possibility.

At this point, a word of caution is called for. The cultural portraits presented so far have been drawn in deliberately bold lines for ease of presentation, yet it needs to be borne in mind that the distinction between collectivist and individualist societies is not categorical, but a matter of degree. There is also much variation to be found within societies as well as between them. For while the centre of gravity of the Chinese cultural ethos lies well within the collectivist sphere, individualism is not completely absent and in certain realms is much admired. Such is the case, for example, with the admiration felt by many who dabble on the Shanghai Stock Exchange towards the unbridled individualism of the wealthy players. This is in large measure precisely because of their success being self-made rather than reliant on family and connections (Hertz 1998). Finding the rugged individualist as hero is not quite what one would expect from notions of the Chinese as governed exclusively by traditional Confucian values, but then values are seldom as simple and unalloyed as the averages to emerge from surveys at times suggest.

Traditional values, moreover, may clash among themselves. Some virtues often considered typically Chinese, such as respect for tradition, concern to protect face and the meticulous reciprocation of greetings, favours and gifts can come into conflict with other equally traditional values such as perseverance and thrift. The former are more oriented to the past or present, the latter to the future. And it is the dynamism of the latter group that has been credited with fuelling Chinese economic success. The Chinese may indeed value tradition and face, but when these conflict with what can be gained by hard work and deferred gratification, they are likely to be sacrificed (Hofstede and Bond 1988). General cultural preferences can also clash with the more pressing claims of self-interest. Questionnaires and simulations in which the Chinese reveal a preference for a more accommodating style of dispute settlement take place in artificial circumstances where little is at stake. However, as we shall see when we come to the negotiations described in the present study, such preferences can soon be pushed aside in favour of a more aggressive stance when substantial matters of self-interest enter into the equation.

Individual values seldom find expression in the same form from one society to another. They always alter according to the broader configuration of values of which they form a part. There is, for example, a general tendency for Chinese communication to be shaped by the desire to avoid open conflict (Gao *et al.* 1996). Open debate requiring direct confrontation tends to be avoided in favour of a more indirect approach. In discussions, the Chinese are likely to preface their own opinion with a review of the common problems and constraints facing all parties. While Westerners may find this unnecessarily vague and diffident, it does serve to reduce the possibility of a polarization of opinion within the group (Young 1982). Norms of Chinese communication stand in direct contrast with the American aversion to ambiguity and preference for plain-speaking (Mead 1990: 132ff.). The Chinese favour the reserved, implicit and indirect (*hanxu*). Consequently, the Chinese are inclined to be constantly on the alert to read between the lines of any message. Nonetheless, this general preference can be offset by other Chinese values. The hierarchical and deferential nature of Chinese society means that those in authority are at liberty to openly berate their subordinates in the bluntest terms and frequently do so, as we shall see.

In many situations, silence is often considered the safest course in a culture that sees the mouth as the fount of misfortune (*huo cong kou shu*). Once again, however, hierarchy enters into the matter. Silence is more golden for some than for others. Children, for example, are expected to be seen and not heard in family gatherings at which adults hold the floor. The good child is one who heeds what s/he is told ('*ting hua* – listens talk') and does not interrupt or talk back. This pattern of superior having the prerogative of speaking and inferior relegated to listening reverently is repeated at school and at work, with acceptance rather than argument expected of students and employees. Consequently, Chinese managers have been found to rate oral fluency as of little importance in their staff (Hildebrandt 1988).

The pursuit of harmony is also linked with traditional Chinese concerns over matters of face. Face serves as the lubricant necessary to sustain harmony among those living in situations where escape is not an option. As Bond and Lee (1981) have argued in discussing face-saving in Hong Kong, face assumes particular importance where the same people meet repeatedly; where identity is derived from group rather than individual activities; and where criticism of superiors is suppressed in favour of knowing one's place.

Under such conditions, so characteristic of Chinese collectivism, attention must be paid to avoiding giving offence. Care must be taken to preserve the face of others. Criticism of others is often phrased in vague or moderate language to avoid loss of face. Similarly, saying 'no' to a request may be interpreted as a not 'giving face'. In this case a rejection may be concealed in an undertaking to consider the matter, or accompanied by excuses to 'pad the face' of the one disappointed. Here also, however, hierarchy is at work in the Chinese context. Face is pre-eminently a matter of power; those in authority have face, while at the same time being free to ignore such considerations in their treatment of subordinates. Those from less hierarchical societies finding themselves in China may misunderstand this aspect of face, as we shall see. Feeling that the concern with social standing and self-esteem to which face relates is universal, they may mistakenly import notions of face as it has been incorporated into their own culture back into their interpretation of Chinese manners.

In speaking of societies in which harmony and forbearance are much in evidence, Colson observes that 'some people live in what appears to be a Rousseauian paradise because they take a Hobbesian view of their situation: they walk softly because they believe it necessary not to offend others whom they regard as dangerous' (Colson 1975: 37). Her remarks could well be applied to China. Traditionally, as Weber notes: 'The Confucian gentleman, striving simply for dignified bearing, distrusted others as generally as he believed others distrusted him' (Weber 1951: 244). This lack of trust in the wider world beyond one's immediate family has led to China being characterized as a low-trust society in contrast to others that are rooted in the Protestant tradition (Fukuyama 2000: 99). This narrow radius of trust has been made much of by Redding in analysing what he sees as the limits on growth of Chinese private enterprises. Among the Chinese, he argues, 'you trust your family absolutely, your friends and acquaintances to the degree that mutual dependence has been established and face invested in them. With everybody else you will make no assumptions about their goodwill' (Redding 1993: 66). Networking and the exchange of favours beyond the family (*guanxi*) relies upon establishing trust, but this trust is specific, limited to partners bound by personal obligations and not by any community of faith. The result is a culture in which nepotism and favouritism are, if not always condoned, at least regarded as in many ways understandable and natural.

So far we have been mainly concerned with values and beliefs. But what do attitudes tell us of behaviour? Has practice matched the value traditionally placed on harmony throughout China's history? Clearly not, for while the clash between ideal and reality is universal, the high ideals and self-sacrifice demanded by Confucianism and communism render admission of the pursuit of self-interest less acceptable than under the private vices–public virtues philosophy of capitalism. The resulting gulf between rhetoric and reality has been so long established and characteristic of Chinese thought that it is taken for granted. This can be seen as far back as in classic works on Chinese imperial military strategy dating from the time of Sun Tzu's *The Art of War* over two thousand years ago. All felt the need to utter pious Confucian platitudes about the efficacy of relying on setting a virtuous example as sufficient to win over neighbouring states before moving on to devote the greater part of their advice to using force and guile to undermine them at every opportunity. The inconsistency was handled adroitly by simply ignoring it (Johnston 1995).

Much the same might be said of contemporary business strategy. In interviews with Chinese managers, one finds oneself frequently hearing descriptions of their business life familiar from official pronouncements. As the interview progresses, however, respondents reaching into their own experience to illustrate their situation almost equally frequently contradict these with equanimity.

Looking back, Hsiao is equally sceptical about whether practice has matched principle in relation to the high value placed on harmony throughout China's history:

> In a society like imperial China, in which discrepancies of interests existed among different segments of the population, in which the administration rarely met the basic needs of the people, and in which ... struggles for subsistence against unfriendly forces of nature and men were normally keen among a large proportion of the inhabitants,

the possibility of conflict was constantly present and social harmony remained more of an ideal than an actuality in everyday life.

(Hsiao 1979: 16)

Only a small number of such conflicts lent themselves to settlement through the courts. This was in part because the written law of pre-modern China was overwhelmingly penal in character. This meant that

> matters of a civil nature were either ignored by it entirely (for example, contracts), or were given only limited treatment within its penal format (for example, property rights, inheritance, marriage). The law was only secondarily interested in defending the rights – especially the economic rights – of one individual or group against another individual or group and not at all in defending such rights against the state . . . If a dispute involved two individuals, individual A did not bring a suit directly against individual B. Rather he lodged his complaint with the authorities who decided whether or not to prosecute individual B.

(Bodde and Morris 1967: 4)

Involvement in the formal system of justice was widely regarded as a road to disaster and therefore to be avoided at all costs. In Confucian thought, law has often been viewed as little more than a necessary evil. As a result, it was not unknown for officials to pen articles strongly advising against resorting to law (Hsiao 1979: 5). Under the Qing code, anyone assisting others to bring a case, whether for a fee or not, was regarded as a troublemaker for inciting litigation and was guilty of a criminal offence (Bodde and Morris 1967: 413–17).

Given the uninviting nature of the law, a number of other forms of social control came to assume greater importance. First, as Hsiao observes, in imperial China 'somewhat greater importance was consistently attached to prevention of conflicts before they arose than to ways and means of resolving them after they had broken out' (Hsiao 1979: 36). One way was through indoctrination. Almost immediately the Qing rulers had consolidated their power, they set about inculcating in the minds of their subjects the virtues of social harmony. Public lectures took place throughout the land, with the first Qing emperor issuing in 1652 'Six Maxims' to be taken as their themes. The third enjoined all subjects 'to maintain harmonious relationships' (Hsiao 1979: 39).

Where preaching proved insufficient, the elders and headmen of local communities were expected to exercise their influence as peacemakers when disputes arose. In addition to the officially recognized local leaders, clans and guilds also provided mechanisms for the resolution of disputes. But perhaps a greater number of disputes were settled outside such institutional arrangements through compromises brokered by individuals mediating in a private capacity (Hsiao 1979: 52). Common to all these methods was an emphasis on bringing the parties to an acceptable compromise, an emphasis foreign to the Chinese law courts with their focus on guilt and punishment.

Many of these practices will strike a chord with those familiar with China in more recent times. Continuing national indoctrination campaigns seeking to instil virtue in the masses through reiteration of a fixed number of slogans are reminiscent of Shi Zu's 'Six Maxims' of over three centuries ago. Government-appointed neighbourhood leaders still step in to act as peacemakers. A reluctance to resort to official court proceedings as a way of settling disputes remains and favours reliance on a range of alternative methods of dispute resolution. Prominent among these is mediation.

The nature of mediation as a means of dispute resolution is best brought out by comparing it with negotiation and adjudication. In negotiation the disputing parties themselves reach a joint decision, in adjudication the decision is made by an authoritative third party. Mediation is more akin to negotiation than adjudication, for while a third party is involved he or she is a facilitator and not an adjudicator. Mediation involves helping people decide for themselves; adjudication involves deciding for them (Gulliver 1979: 209–10).

Current Chinese law continues the tradition of discouraging formal litigation in most cases except as a last resort. A great number of Chinese laws and regulations provide negotiation as a preliminary method for settling disputes followed in order by mediation, arbitration and litigation (Mo 1997: 368–9). Wang attributes the continuity of these traditional patterns to the fact that most of the leaders involved in founding the People's Republic were from the countryside and were accustomed to the traditional idea of resolving disputes through compromise (Wang 1993: 525).

The courts can use mediation in most civil cases. In addition to the tradition of settling disputes by mediation, it also appears likely that, particularly in rural areas, there are political pressures on the courts that lead them to favour this approach. A report by the Supreme Court speaks of local cadres who, displeased with the prospect of having to repay debts owed to members of another community,

> may even obstruct the court from accepting a case or reaching a verdict or enforcing an order. . . . During the past two years more than eighty court cadres and bailiffs have been beaten up and injured when carrying out their tasks, and some have even died in the line of duty.
>
> (Quoted in Palmer 1991: 226)

In such circumstances, Palmer comments, 'a mediated compromise agreement – rather than a clear-cut adjudication – helps to fudge the issue, saves the continuing and important Chinese commodity of "face" (*mianzi*) and avoids alienating seriously the losing party (who may be very influential at the local level)' (Palmer 1991: 226).

Foreign companies attempting to enforce awards in their favour made by the China International Economic and Trade Arbitration Commission (CIETAC), China's international arbitral body, have encountered similar difficulties. Although under the Civil Procedure Law a Chinese People's Court is bound to enforce a CIETAC award except in very limited circumstances, they have sometimes shown reluctance to do so against Chinese parties. As Moser explains, 'this is mainly because enforcement decisions are rendered by local courts at the place where the assets of the defendant are located. Such courts are especially vulnerable to political and economic pressures from local authorities and interested parties' (Moser 1995: 247).

The CIETAC also places a high value in attempting to mediate the dispute before it rather than proceeding directly to adjudication:

> In practice, this means that once the issues have been defined in the hearing, the arbitrators will often encourage the parties to attempt to resolve their dispute by compromise and mutual accommodation. . . . This distinctive Chinese approach to arbitration is reasonable in theory, but it can at times entail problems if a party insists upon its 'legal rights'. Such a party may be viewed by the arbitrators as uncompromising and unreasonable, with the result that the award which it has insisted upon may turn out to be less favourable than it envisaged.
>
> (Moser 1995: 246)

Turning from the law to how organizations diagnose and remedy internal conflicts we encounter wide variation. Discussing cross-cultural comparisons of how managers diagnose the causes of inter-departmental conflict, Hofstede (1994: 139ff.) makes use of dimensions identified in the Aston studies to distinguish organizations according to their degree of concentration of authority and the extent to which activities are structured. Nations differ in terms of their preferred form of organization as measured on these dimensions, as illustrated in Figure 2.2. Given a dispute between two departmental heads, different nationalities are likely to approach its resolution in different ways. The French, for example, are likely to identify the source of the conflict as negligence on the part of the manager to whom the two departmental heads report. The solution is for them to submit the matter to their common boss. The form of organization advocated here has a highly structured hierarchy, a classic bureaucracy. The Germans, on the other hand, are likely to identify the problem as resulting from a lack of structure. The solution then lies in the elaboration of rules. The British are unlikely to identify the source of the problem as due to insufficient concentration of authority or lack of rules. For them it is more likely to be seen as a human relations problem, with the two departmental heads in need of training as to how to get along together. An ad hoc solution dictated by the situation at hand, rather than by appeals to procedure or reference upwards, is sought.

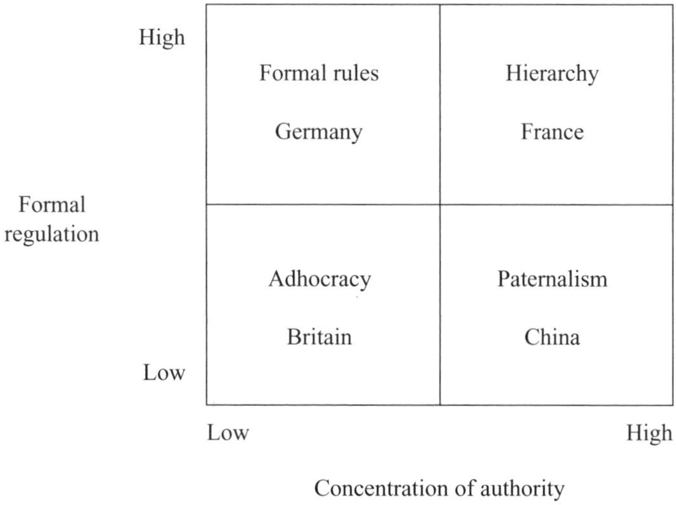

High	Formal rules Germany	Hierarchy France
Formal regulation	Adhocracy Britain	Paternalism China
Low		

Low   High

Concentration of authority

Figure 2.2 Organizational models
Source: based on Hofstede (1994: 140ff.)

The fourth preferred form of organization is one in which conflicts are resolved by constant referral to a boss running an organization in which procedures and duties are not clearly defined by rules. The organization is viewed much as an extended family ruled in a paternalistic manner. This is frequently regarded as typical of Chinese organizations. As can be seen from Figure 2.2, this places the national preferences of the two joint venture owners of the exhibition centre in this study in diametrically opposed quadrants. The expectation might well be that the German side would place its faith in written agreements to handle conflict, while the Chinese side might be expected to be constantly reliant on higher authority to settle disputes with little reference to formal agreements. We shall see later how far this turns out to be true.

That Chinese firms are high in the concentration of power and lack the structure provided by clearly established rules has long been characteristic of most overseas Chinese enterprises. The great majority of these are small family-owned businesses (Redding 1993: 146). The boss keeps a tight hold on the reins of authority, partly as the result of a lack of trust in anyone beyond the family circle. This, Redding claims, is firmly rooted in Chinese culture and acts as a brake on company expansion. However, in his study of Taiwanese businesses, Hwang (1990) argues that Chinese firms are not fated to be shackled by culture in this way. His account shows that larger Taiwanese firms in the private sector that are not family owned have successfully moved away from traditional practices. Values such as paternalism and filial piety have been replaced as organizing principles by others such as the use of clear company regulations. In this the firms were more similar to American-owned companies on the island than to Chinese family-owned businesses. Large state-owned firms in Taiwan, however, compared rather poorly in this respect.

The same is true of state-owned companies in the People's Republic, which have typically combined a concentration of power with the absence of clearly defined responsibilities. The result has been rather unkindly characterized as one in which 'the critical art is to avoid responsibility, diffuse decisions, and blunt all commands that might later leave one vulnerable to criticisms' (Pye 1982: 16). This situation is changing as a result of the reforms, but unevenly (Guthrie 1999). It often remains the case that solving problems can be a slow affair as matters are passed upwards for decision. The multitude of bureaux that impinge on the way a firm operates can complicate matters further and add to delays. The reputation of large Chinese organizations as unusually slow in reaching decisions may be compounded by the Chinese preference for waiting on the achievement of consensus within peer groups rather than pushing ahead on the basis of a simple majority (Yates and Lee 1996: 346). In such circumstances it is perhaps not surprising that when a group of Chinese managers were given hypothetical situations in which they had to solve problems through negotiation with Chinese and Canadian firms, they, like the Canadians, considered that negotiations with the latter would be more satisfying and easier to control (Tse *et al.* 1994).

When Chinese and foreigners work together within the same enterprise expectations may well clash concerning the appropriate structure and operation of the organization. In his comparison of Chinese and American co-workers in a privately owned restaurant in China, Yu (1995), for example, found marked differences in cultural assumptions about work roles. The owner took an active role in overseeing the business, but also employed two managers, one Chinese, the other American. The waiters were both Chinese and American. The Chinese staff viewed the managers as having little autonomy, their role being simply to convey the directions of the owner. Perceived as having little authority, the Chinese workers would often go over the manager's head by approaching the owner directly should any problem arise. The Chinese manager seemed to concur with this assessment of his position, and in general played a fairly passive role. The American manager, in contrast, saw the post as entailing a responsibility to take a much more active role. This included devising ways to improve the running of the business and putting them into operation. In adopting this role, he met with no resistance from the American staff, who considered it his duty. The Chinese employees, on the other hand, resented being told what to do when they suspected the instructions did not come from the owner himself, often checking with him. The proprietor was himself rather taken aback by the zeal of his American manager, commenting that he did too much. The American workers, on the other hand, were critical of their Chinese colleagues for not listening to the manager, and of the owner for not giving him enough responsibility and support. We shall see similar differences in outlook at work on the project.

Continuity and change

Given the evidence for differences between China and many Western countries in the way conflict is approached, the question remains as to how persistent such differences are likely to prove. Much depends on the relative weight attributed to cultural, political and economic factors in shaping business systems and managerial practices. Are the differences rooted in age-old traditional beliefs and values, too deeply embedded to be easily displaced (Hofstede 1980; Trompenaars 1993)? Are the differences we see in management of more recent origin, stemming from the days of a fully planned economy (Child and Markóczy 1994)? Or do we need to look to the enduring mark left on institutions by the unique configuration of national and international circumstances prevailing at the time of their creation (Dore 1990)? Do the various institutional factors combine to form a distinctive national business system to which firms have to adapt (Whitley 1992)? Or are these forces that foster difference being overwhelmed by pressure towards worldwide convergence in business practices brought on by the competitive pressures inherent in globalization?

The balance between such forces is not the same everywhere. Those features of firms linked closely to the capital market or constrained by technology and economies of scale are more likely to show convergence. Below these strategic, macro-level issues the style of management adopted in such areas as decision-making, communication, trust and conflict management may well have greater freedom to vary with local preferences and to accommodate local institutions (Child 1981).

More broadly, can traditional Chinese values, such as collectivism with its stress on harmony, survive in the face of modernization? There are broadly two schools of thought on this question. One sees core Chinese cultural values as deeply embedded in traditions that have survived thousands of years. As such, they are unlikely to be casually cast aside. Others have argued that China's traditional culture was the product of an agricultural society and that as Chinese communities become more industrialized they will abandon outdated values. An example of this approach can be found in the early work of Yang (1986). Surveying findings from numerous psychological studies that mainly centred on comparisons between Chinese and Americans, he concluded that the former were indeed more likely to display social harmoniousness, group-mindedness and mutual dependency. However, he also noted that evidence from Taiwan suggests that its inhabitants are moving away from such a social orientation towards a more individualistic one. This he attributed to the rapid industrialization of Taiwan favouring such characteristics. The implications are clear. Given industrialization, Chinese people will become much like other members of advanced industrial societies.

Responding to critics of modernization theory, Yang later came to regard this approach as oversimplified. His earlier view assumed that modern values are all the polar opposites of traditional values so that if you have more of one you inevitably get less of the other. It also treated values as all tied to each other and moving in unison. However, many traditional values continue to exist alongside modern ones. Reviewing evidence from more recent Chinese studies Yang was led to conclude that 'some collectivist and individualistic characteristics may coexist in persons in a modern society, and the former need not be eventually replaced by the latter through the process of societal modernization' (Yang 1996: 492).

It is interesting with respect to this problem to look at Hong Kong in comparison with mainland China and the United States, as Hong Kong residents are betwixt and between in exposure to both Western and Eastern influences. When asked, 79 per cent of respondents in Hong Kong reported themselves Westernized in some respects, while at the same time 71 per cent considered themselves as being Chinese with regard to other aspects of their character (Bond and King 1985). Looking specifically at the values held by managers in the three locations, Ralston and his colleagues confirmed this picture of Hong Kong. It was found to mix influences from both China and the West, occupying a point midway between the two with regard to some values, such as thrift and perseverance, while holding firm to the Chinese pattern with regard to others, such as placing a greater emphasis on trust and personal relations over contracts (Ralston *et al.* 1993).

Goody makes a similar point to that of Yang in arguing against the supposed greater rationality of the West in comparison with the East. Part of the problem he sees as misusing rationality to qualify people or cultures as a whole, rather than some of their actions some of the time. In the West as well as the East 'what happens on Sundays does not necessarily control daily behaviour . . . even computer operators may believe in the Dao, in Buddha, in the Christian Trinity, or in transcendental meditation' (Goody 1996: 45).

Goody argues against modernization theories that see development as the wholesale abandonment of one set of practices in favour of another. In its place he argues for a conception of development as the broadening of the available repertoire. Thus, the economy does not move from one of family firms to one of bureaucratic corporations, but to one in which both are present.

Rowe (1984) makes a similar point in the course of arguing against Weber's claim that the Chinese city lacked a sense of communal identity as inhabitants looked constantly to their place of origin as the source of their loyalties. In his study of nineteenth-century Hankow, Rowe shows that place of origin did indeed feature largely as a way of cementing relationships. Yet he goes on to demonstrate that such identities did not exclude a further one as a Hankow citizen. Which identity was uppermost depended on circumstances. Such multiplication of social identities rather than their substitution is common and not confined to China. One need only think of the role of ethnic identities in America. When looking at conflict, it is frequently sensible to approach identity less as a matter of 'what are they?' and more as a matter of 'when are they?'*

The whole question of convergence is intriguing, not least because we often do not know enough about both sides to begin with. Sometimes the gap between China and the West is wider than it seems. Paying lip-service to shared principles may hide differences in practice. Sometimes the gap is less than it appears. This can happen when we fail to compare like with like, with observers comparing the principles of their own society with the practices of another. Much is made, for example, of the Chinese reluctance to rely on the law to settle disputes. Yet, such a position is not unknown to the West. In his study of the degree to which litigation was used to settle disputes between American firms, Macaulay notes that disputes are

> frequently settled without reference to the contract or potential or actual legal sanctions. . . . as one businessman put it, 'You can settle any dispute if you keep the lawyers and accountants out of it. They just do not understand the give-and-take needed in business.' . . . Law suits for breach of contract appear to be rare.
>
> (1963: 61)

And speaking in terms that would not sound out of place applied to China he goes on to note:

> Even where agreement can be reached at the negotiation stage, carefully planned arrangements may create undesirable exchange relationships between business units. Some businessmen object that in such a carefully worked out relationship one gets performance only to the letter of the contract. Such planning indicates a lack of trust and blunts the demands of friendship, turning a cooperative venture into an antagonistic horse trade.
>
> (Macaulay 1963: 63)

In China's transition to a market-oriented economy, enormous changes are underway. But the path that China is treading is in many ways unique, shaped by its own pre-existing institutional structures. Walder, for example,

---

* In deciding which identity to assert or play down, self-interest naturally plays a part. As the landlord in the film *My Beautiful Launderette* answers in reply to an appeal to his ethnic sympathies to go easy on his tenants: 'I am a professional businessman, not a professional Pakistani.'

has commented on how China's reforms are highly path dependent, shaped by the position from which it entered upon reform. From the outset of the transition its industrial hierarchies were already more decentralized than those in the former Soviet Union and vastly larger than those of the smaller communist countries (Walder 1995).

Guthrie (1999) has argued that how a state firm reacts to change reflects the position it held in China's industrial hierarchy:

> Ironically, it is the firms that were the most protected in the planned economy – those at the upper levels of the administrative hierarchy (e.g., firms directly under the jurisdiction of bureaux) – that are experiencing the greatest sense of uncertainty and abandonment . . . while those furthest from the central government are experiencing a more partial or gradual reform.
>
> (Guthrie 1999: 40)

It is this experience of uncertainty and abandonment, he argues, that fuels the enthusiasm for adopting more formal management practices.

In many changes there is clearly an element of imitation of foreign models. But such imitation is no mere passive matter. It often has a large element of selection, borrowing aspects from one model and mixing these with another according to China's particular circumstances. Warner and Ng have commented on how the pattern of selective adoption has been shaped by political needs:

> The 1995 codification of the Labour Law and the conscious propagation of the collective contract as one of its key provisions are overtly emulative attempts by the PRC to benchmark its evolving labour market(s) at home against those which have been established in the mature capitalist economies like Euro-American and Japan. However, as the late-developers, China now enjoys a strategic advantage in having latitude of choice and adaptation to a variety of alternative versions of putting collective bargaining to practice. Obviously, what China has formulated and yielded from its (institutional) drawing board is a 'hybrid' product mixing both Western and Eastern flavour, plus its own imaginative and innovative inputs so as to harmonize activities of 'collective bargaining' with the politico-economic needs of the socialist-cum-capitalist workplace now featuring China.
>
> (Warner and Ng 1998: 28)

This is one area where the foreign-funded sector in China has not been a leading light for reform:

> Actually many of these multi-national corporations have not been receptive to their own home-made institutions like trade unions and

collective bargaining. Indeed, the 'China' domain could have afforded them, in their calculations, with an escape away from the 'tyranny' of the western regime of industrial regulation pivoted around these enshrined institutions.

(Warner and Ng 1998: 24–5)

When talking of the values of managers in today's China, we need to take the diversity within their ranks into account. It must be borne in mind that many of China's provinces are larger in both area and population than many countries in Europe. Geographical barriers that have resulted in a large number of mutually incomprehensible dialects separate them. Movement between them has been restricted for much of the communist era by a system of residence permits that has only recently begun to loosen its grip. The provinces are also different in terms of history and economic resources and development. These all find reflection in differences in business ethos between the localities. Managers in the thriving coastal cities of Shanghai and Guangzhou, for example, tend to be far more individualistic in their openness to change and unabashed pursuit of individual self-interest than those encountered in the more remote and less developed inland cities of Chengdu and Lanzhou (Ralston *et al.* 1996).

Consideration also needs to be given to a growing generation gap. As one might expect, the new generation of managers, those in their twenties and thirties who have spent a greater proportion of their upbringing and professional lives in the era of reform, are more individualistic than their elders. Living in a world that has altered so dramatically, from one of planning and the mentality of the iron rice bowl to one of market forces and the glorification of getting rich, has naturally had an impact.

Even the younger generation of managers is still, however, far more collectivist in approach than its American counterpart (Ralston *et al.* 1993; 1999). Insofar as attitudes towards authority are rooted in patterns of upbringing within the family it would be unwise to expect such differences to fade into insignificance, for traditional patterns of child-rearing by Chinese parents are resilient to change. Even among the third generation of Chinese immigrants to America, child-rearing patterns remain distinct from the rest of the population through adherence to traditional Chinese virtues (Wu 1996: 154).

Much of the present chapter has been concerned with what is distinctive about Chinese values and how they may impinge upon management practices. There can be no doubt that values do play a part here, but they are not the only factor in the equation. If management practices in China are compared with those in Hungary under communist rule, for example, a number of striking similarities emerge in areas such as decision-making, communication and personnel practices. Compared to their counterparts in advanced capitalist countries managers in both exhibit a reluctance to make decisions and an inclination to shift responsibility and blame on to others.

As for communication, they are unwilling to share information, failing to pass this on to their subordinates or other departments. A great deal of paperwork is generated in the form of reports and signed authorizations, usually more for protecting managers from blame than furthering the effective operation of the enterprise. In the personnel area they stand in contrast with advanced capitalist countries in their lack of effective systems for hiring, firing and rewarding staff (Child and Markóczy 1994).

Obviously, these similarities are not attributable to any shared familiarity with the Confucian classics. What they do appear to share in common is a shared system of state ownership and control of industry. This system produces the defensive behaviour outlined earlier through the dependence of managers on cultivating good relations with officials outside the enterprise and political organs within it. Here, then, it appears to be more the logic of the situation in which managers find themselves than traditional values that determine their behaviour. The implication is that managers from other cultures placed in their shoes might soon find themselves constrained by the institutional setting to operate in a similar manner. We shall encounter such slippage at work on the project and look into the circumstances that shape its progress.

Construction

When it comes to conflict, certain industries are more prone to it than others by the very nature of the work they undertake. Construction is one. As Higgin and Jessop remark:

> If, as is usually the case, there are several members of the building team sharing the work of constructing the brief, any one of them, but particularly the one in the role of sponsor, can unbalance the whole by a too single-minded pursuit of perfection for those aspects that are his especial concern. The architect/sponsor, for example, will be tempted to maximize architectural magnificence at the expense of time, cost, or technological considerations, the quantity surveyor/sponsor to maximize economy at the expense of architectural or technological considerations, and the builder/sponsor to maximize profit at the expense of architecture and client's financial outlay.
>
> (Higgin and Jessop 1965: 19–20)

Intertwined with this clash of interests, communication can also be a problem:

A comment from one builder:-

> 'I do find quite frequently when I go on to a site that the poor wretched foreman, who has no access to contract drawings and

things that may be filed away in a safe, is just building from the wrong drawings, How is he to know? . . .'

This, however, is not a situation which builders find universally disadvantageous.

'I for one would not be at all put out if I found my foreman working to a set of drawings totally different from the contract drawings. I would start sharpening my pencil and think up all the extras I could claim as a consequence. It is on these items that we make our money.'

(Higgin and Jessop 1965: 33)

Disagreements over matters of fact are made more difficult to resolve as they are frequently anchored in an underlying conflict of interest, as Clegg's description of an argument on a construction site in Britain over what constitutes 'normal clay' illustrates (Clegg 1975). The difference was over the foundation of a building that was designed to be built on what the architects regarded as normal clay. However, the interpretation of the term by the civil engineering contractor was influenced by the fact that it could charge the client for removal of extra earth. This led to a much stricter interpretation of 'normal clay' by the earth excavator operator, one that naturally suited its interests.

The classic problem from which transaction cost economics developed was the question of whether to make or buy, to produce in-house or to purchase from outside. The choice lies between the relative costs and benefits of hierarchy and the market. Large and innovative construction projects are frequently faced with the likelihood of changing client specifications as the work progresses; uncertainty of costs; and great difficulty in monitoring performance. All these factors raise the transaction cost of obtaining satisfactory performance from other firms. They thus would appear to argue against market provision in favour of the advantages offered by the hierarchy provided by the firm. However, most clients are in construction for such a short time as to make this impractical. One solution to this dilemma, and one frequently encountered in the construction industry, is to create contracts that bind firms together in a fashion that mimics the essential elements of hierarchy to be found within the firm. To create such a hierarchy a contract will have to outline an authority system integrating the contractors and client through such measures as an intricate array of approval procedures, provisions allowing change orders to be issued by the engineer representing the client, and the institution of routine dispute resolution procedures (Stinchcombe and Heimer 1985: 121–69).

Quite how successful a particular arrangement will be depends in part on its cultural context. In England, for example, construction contracts frequently charge the engineer with interim interpretation of the contract in the case of a dispute between the contractor and the client. This is defended on the basis that, although the client employs the engineer, s/he is an independent professional who will give an objective interpretation of the contract. However, as Stinchcombe remarks,

> In England itself this usually works to resolve the dispute – when the contract language is exported abroad it tends to result in interim client dictatorship through the Engineer's agency, because professional institutions protecting the Engineer's autonomy are not well developed elsewhere.
>
> (Stinchcombe and Heimer 1985: 163)

How do attempts fare in China to use the contract to fashion a new unity out of elements of the client organization and the project contractor? Let us see.

Part II

3 Background to the project

The city of Weserstein is renowned for the trade fairs and exhibitions it hosts. It was on a visit to one of these in 1998 that Wang Ke, the deputy general manager of the special zone Land Development Corporation of a large coastal city in China, approached the organizer of the exhibition, Weserstein Fair. He was interested in exploring the possibility of a cooperative venture aimed at establishing an exhibition centre in the special development zone.

The special development zone is an area of the city that was designated one of China's special economic zones by the central government in the 1990s. It was then largely an undeveloped rural area at a distance from the historic industrial and commercial heart of the city. The government's ambition was to develop the zone into an international financial and trade centre, one that would allow the city to rival Hong Kong and Singapore as a leading regional centre of finance and commerce. To lay the foundation for this, great attention was focused on creating an impressive infrastructure to serve as an attractive window of investment into China. The special zone was to be developed as a location for major international meetings and fairs. The result has been a futuristic skyline to rival any modern metropolis rising from what had previously been a flat expanse of paddy fields. This has been achieved within the past ten years, a period in which, according to the statistics of the special zone government, a new building of over thirty floors was being completed every twelve days. As with many official figures in China, one is tempted to exercise a degree of caution, but no one visiting the area can fail to admire the scale of the achievement.

The Land Development Corporation was set up in the early 1990s as one of two land developers owned by the city government with responsibility for leasing land within the special zone. As with many other organizational innovations throughout the reform period, the intention was to move away from straightforward planning by government bureaucrats towards creating an independent organization that was to benefit from the guiding hand of commercial considerations. Nevertheless, the interconnections between the Land Development Corporation and the local government remain labyrinthine. Most of the senior- and middle-level managers are from government bureaux. The local government provided the corporation with the initial capital to pay for land, which the corporation could lease for development once it had resettled farmers and installed basic utilities. The money earned in this way was expected to be devoted to further developing infrastructure in the special zone according to the government plan; building roads, underground, bridges, parks etc. The Land Development Corporation was allocated all the land in the special zone apart from the Jinrong financial centre. By 2000, the Land Development Corporation had leased out most of its land and was casting around for new sources of income to ensure its survival. Running exhibitions was viewed as one such source.

This fitted well with the plans for the special zone. One area of the special zone under the responsibility of the Land Development Corporation had long been designated in the government plan as a cultural district. The district was intended as home to a science and technology museum, an art and theatre centre, and an exhibition centre, as well as playing host to a major international fair for which the city was bidding in the event of success. It was against this background that the approach by the Land Development Corporation to Weserstein Fair took place.

It occurred at a time when the European market for trade fairs was becoming increasingly saturated. Facing fierce competition, German fair companies were eager to search for new markets outside Europe. China was one possibility. Both Weserstein Fair and Altdurf Fair had opened sales offices in the city to recruit exhibitors for their fairs located outside China. Through the operation of these offices, they had some knowledge of the exhibition industry in China, a relatively immature and segmented market, with around 1,200 exhibitions at the national level staged each year. The exhibitions are repetitive and of low quality. Apart from what they saw as their competitive advantage, the German fair companies were also preoccupied with fears that rivals might enter and establish a position that would make later entry difficult.

The stage seemed set for a mutually beneficial partnership. In addition to the interests of the Land Development Corporation, the city government was also keen to make the city the exhibition centre of East Asia. It viewed the German fair companies, particularly Weserstein Fair, as possessing the necessary expertise and financial resources to bring this about.

However, despite the idea of developing an international exhibition centre fitting in with Weserstein's strategy, Weserstein Fair did not want to take the risk on its own. It therefore approached two major competitors, Rhernseld Fair and Altdurf Fair. The three companies are more or less evenly matched. Weserstein Fair was founded over fifty years ago. It has over one million square metres of exhibition space in twenty-seven halls. In 2000, it employed 700 staff and had total revenue of DM647 million, with a profit of DM96 million. In the same year, it organized seventy-three fairs and exhibitions in Germany and abroad. Its subsidiary,

Weserstein Fair International was established in the mid-1980s. It oversees the group's operations abroad, including Shanghai and Hong Kong. In recent years, Weserstein Fair has built on average a new hall every year.

Altdurf Fair was founded in the mid-1940s, the state in which it is situated owning 56 per cent of the shares, with the rest owned privately. It has seventeen halls compromising over 230 thousand square metres of exhibition space. It employed around 600 staff in 2000 with total sales of DM660 million and a profit of DM29 million. In Asia, Altdurf Fair has subsidiaries in Singapore, Japan, Korea, China and India.

Rhernseld Fair was established in the mid-1960s. It has sixteen exhibition halls providing 160 thousand square metres of exhibition space. It organizes about forty trade fairs each year. In Asia, Rhernseld has a subsidiary in Singapore.

The three companies agreed to form a strategic alliance to enter the Chinese market. This was to take the form of a joint venture among the German partners, to be called German Fair. This was established in April 1999, with each of the three owning a third of the shares. Its main mission was to establish a Sino-German alliance to build and run an exhibition centre in China. Previously the three trade fair companies had operated independently in Asia, but German Fair offered the opportunity to pool strengths, and to share the risks and financial burdens of entering a new market.

Negotiating the joint venture

The Germans were not the only ones trying to grasp such an opportunity. Other international players such as the British company Mayfair were also interested in establishing a similar venture. While German Fair was negotiating with the Land Development Corporation, Mayfair was talking to another Chinese state-owned company about establishing an exhibition centre in the city. However, German Fair succeeded in stopping this and obtained a written promise from the city government about not building another permanent exhibition centre in the city. The government asked Mayfair to join German Fair as another partner. However, Mayfair pulled out when it ran into financial difficulties.

The negotiation of the joint venture between German Fair and the Land Development Corporation was difficult and lengthy. Among other obstacles, the partners could not decide upon the division of shares, with both parties insisting on taking the majority. The Germans wished from the beginning to secure a majority shareholding. However, as this touched upon ownership of a major public facility by a foreign firm, the Chinese side were unwilling to concede. The involvement of state ownership on both sides exacerbated the difficulty of negotiating a major joint venture. Major decisions had to await agreement by both Chinese and German officials. In addition, the German partners were geographically separated, further prolonging decision-making on their side.

However, the end of 1999 saw agreement on an equal division of the shares between the German and Chinese sides, with neither partner holding a majority. The joint venture was to be known as the International Exhibition Centre. Its mission was to build and operate an exhibition complex in the special zone. The structure of the joint venture is illustrated in Figure 3.1. The contribution of the Land Development Corporation to the joint venture was through the provision of the land. German Fair contributed by providing finance for the construction and operation of the exhibition centre. The city government arranged to have three Chinese state banks provide a loan to German Fair for the construction phase and the initial operating phase at an annual interest rate of 6.1 per cent. The board was to consist of six directors contributed equally by the two sides. The chair was to be taken by one of the directors appointed by the Land Development Corporation. The general manager of the joint venture was to be nominated by German Fair and the deputy general manager by the Land Development Corporation. Decisions on the daily operation of the joint venture were to be made by the two managers jointly. German Fair nominated a German, Steinhausen, as general manager. He has degrees in oriental studies from both German and Chinese universities and is fluent in Mandarin. Steinhausen had also worked in a German investment bank on China-related projects for over fifteen years. Zhang Haiying was nominated by the Land Development Corporation to be deputy general manager. She had been transferred to the Land Development Corporation from the municipal government, where she was an official working in the foreign economic and trade commission with responsibility for organizing international trade fairs. The target date for completion of phase one of the project was to be the end of July 2001, in order to host a prestigious high-tech fair in September of

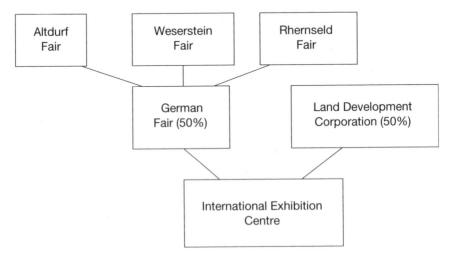

Figure 3.1 The structure of the joint venture

that year. It was hoped that Premier Zhu Rongji and Chancellor Schroeder would open this jointly.

The architect

The partners agreed to employ Young and Muller to design the project. Owned by one of the world's leading architects, the American-based firm was no stranger to contributing to the futurist skyline of the city, having been involved in the design of other buildings there for over ten years. The design it proposed envisaged the exhibition centre comprising, in its final form, seventeen exhibition halls, a congress centre and a hotel. The halls form a triangle, with entries in between, creating a large triangular centre, which serves as an open exhibition area. The repeating structures of the halls form a soft wave, intended to give the project a unique image and to make it one of the landmarks in the city. Phase one of the construction project was to build four of the exhibition halls and the entrance hall, comprising an area of forty-five thousand square metres of indoor exhibition space with a further twenty thousand square metres available on open-air sites. The investment for phase one was to be $99 million.

Anke, a German structural engineering and design consultancy, undertook the structural design. Anke has a long-running working relationship with Young and Muller, with Anke's designs characterized by load-bearing structures that have been reduced to the absolute minimum, with large areas of glass to render the structures transparent and well lit. By applying new joint and assembly techniques, it is able to build roofs of large spans that maintain an appearance of filigree-like lightness. In addition to it being an architectural highlight, the centre was designed to be the most modern and most efficient of its kind in East Asia. Another German firm, Interstall, was given charge of the mechanical and electrical design with this in mind. The architectural input was indisputably first class by international standards. Only by bearing in mind the high hopes and sums invested in the design can the extent of the frustration that lay behind a number of the subsequent conflicts be appreciated.

The Chinese government insists that foreign designs have to comply with Chinese standards and regulations, which frequently differ from international norms in place elsewhere in the world. According to both Western and Chinese architects that I have spoken to, Chinese standards and regulations for building design are highly conservative. They were drawn up in the 1950s, bringing together the most conservative criteria from a number of different national codes. They have remained largely unchanged ever since without accommodating changing construction methods and improvements in the quality of materials.

Foreign architects and designers have to retain the services of Chinese state-owned design institutes as consultants on Chinese standards and regulations. Young and Muller therefore employed City Modern Architectural

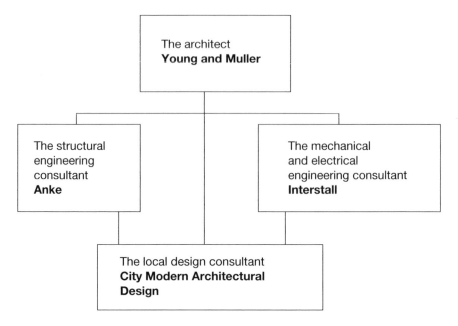

Figure 3.2 The architect and the engineering and design consultants

Design (CMAD), a state-owned design institute with the highest state classification (see Figure 3.2).

The project management team

Although foreign architects design most of the city's impressive skyline, foreign project management services are limited to projects directly invested by foreign companies or Sino-foreign joint ventures with a majority shareholding held by the foreign partners. German Fair insisted upon employing the services of an international project management company, while the Land Development Corporation favoured the traditional Chinese state enterprise approach of managing the project through its own management team. A compromise was finally reached under which a collaborative project management team was set up, with Moreland nominated by German Fair as its representative. This was to be balanced by a Chinese team nominated by the Land Development Corporation. The situation is illustrated in Figure 3.3. The project management team took the shape of a contractual joint venture with equal decision-making power. Ma Bo, a manager from the project management department of the Land Development Corporation, took the title of project manager. Martin Li, a senior project manager from Moreland, took up the title of deputy project manager.

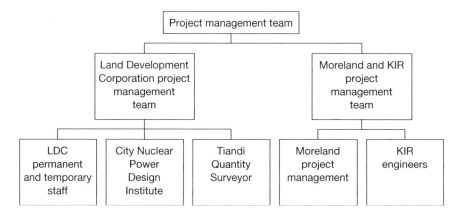

Figure 3.3 The project management team

Moreland is one of the world's leading project management and construction services companies. Moreland has been in the city since 1993, when it became involved in two projects. One was a small consulting job on the then important Stock Exchange. The other was a city water treatment plant, a twenty-year build, operate and transfer scheme constructed and managed jointly with a British utility company and costing in the region of $73 million. The latter project was regarded in 1993 as both risky and high profile. That Moreland was prepared to undertake it was welcomed by the government, which allowed Moreland to keep its construction licence, design qualification certificate and general contractor licence, all of which are difficult for a foreign firm to obtain. However, up to the year 2000, most of Moreland's clients were multinationals. These were preferred because, in the words of one Moreland manager, 'we can talk and understand each other. They will understand the legality of the contract and will pay us.' Nevertheless, Moreland China was appointed by the Chinese government as one of the consultants for China's bid for the Olympic games in 2008, based on Moreland Australia having provided the Australian government with management services for the Sydney Olympics.

Moreland heard about the International Exhibition Centre project through its former parent company, Mayfair. However, German Fair's first nominee as its project management representative was KIR, a German firm. KIR, however, was unable to obtain the necessary licence to undertake projects in China. KIR decided to give the project to Moreland on condition that the latter employed two of KIR's staff on the project management team, one a cost engineer, the other a mechanical engineer.

For its side of the project management team, the Land Development Corporation nominated two of its staff members, one the project manager,

Ma Bo, and the other a structural engineer, Mao Yaming. The rest of the Chinese side of the team came from two outside organizations. The cost engineers were provided by Tiandi, partly owned by CMAD and partly owned by the managers and staff of Tiandi themselves. The mechanical, electrical and hydraulic engineers came from the City Nuclear Power Design Institute. They generally attributed the involvement of their institute in the project as being due to one of their colleagues being the sister of an official in charge of regulating the local construction industry.

The quality supervisor

Chinese building regulations require, in addition to the project management team, the appointment of Jianli, a quality supervisor, to inspect work on the project to ensure that it meets quality standards. This tended to be regarded by the Moreland team as somewhat superfluous, given their own presence: 'Something I do not understand, but something we have to have,' as one of their senior project managers replied to my enquiry about the role of the quality supervisor on the project.

The puzzlement of the Moreland team sprang from a duplication of the service they themselves were undertaking on behalf of the owner. Duplication on the project was, however, to be a recurring theme. It was rooted in two principal sources. First, as we have seen with the division of the project management team, there was a tendency within the joint venture to perpetuate divisions down into the structure rather than resolving them. Second, there is a general tendency within the Chinese state bureaucracy towards a proliferation of supervisory bodies when problems occur. If someone or some body is not doing a job well, the answer is to set someone to watch over them. The overall effect, however, is often to disperse responsibility over a range of different bodies so that ultimate responsibility is difficult to locate and easy to evade.

Two quality supervisor companies were employed. One, Keyi, was given specific responsibility for the steel structure, and the other, Dayu, general responsibility for the whole project. Both are offshoots of government bureaux and institutes in the construction field. They are *minying* companies, companies partly owned by their parent bureau, partly by the staff themselves.

The decision to use a general contractor

The Land Development Corporation and its project management team favoured the traditional practice of employing specialist trades directly. This, according to informants, including some from the Land Development Corporation, is partly traditional, but more importantly the decision makers can get kickbacks from dealing with more contractors rather than operating through one general contractor and the managers can use the opportunity to extend their business networks. The German partners preferred to employ a general contractor in the hope that they would only have to hold one company to account for quality, schedule and a guaranteed price. In a country in which business practices and the legal system were unfamiliar, the German partners wanted to limit the number of local companies they would have to deal with to the absolute minimum. German Fair eventually won this battle and the stage was set for tendering to commence.

4 Tendering

The choice facing the owners was not simply either to supervise the construction directly or to appoint a general contractor to do everything on their behalf. There was a middle way, albeit one leaning more towards the general contractor option. This was to appoint some of the principal subcontractors directly, later assigning these to the general contractor as part of the latter's contract. The owners decided upon this route.

The main structure of the building was to be of steel. The owner chose to retain the right to appoint the firm that was to be responsible for fabricating and erecting the steel structure rather than leaving this to the discretion of the general contractor once appointed. This would provide savings, as the price of locally available steel was rising. It would also cut down on the time needed for construction. Early appointment of the steel fabricator would also have the advantage of enabling it to press ahead with solving production problems posed by the innovatory design. One possible disadvantage of this route, however, was noted in a report to the owners from the Moreland project manager: 'In practice, no matter how carefully the contract document has been detailed, the nominated subcontractor always leads to more disputes with the general contractor and greater responsibility on the Owner.'

The solicitor for German Fair shared these reservations. He advised against the owner nominating a subcontractor, suggesting this was better left in the hands of the general contractor. In a letter, the attorney advised 'in our opinion a basic (often ignored) principle of lawyers should be "if possible, keep it simple."' In line with this principle, he advised wariness of the nominated subcontractor approach on the basis that it made contractual arrangements more complex and increased the risk of disputes. The attorney also drew on his firm's practical experience in China to warn that resort to arbitration was rare, however clearly regulated in the contract. The result was that contracts were left to interpretation by non-lawyers involved in the construction as the contractors sought to make claims and to blame one another for delays. This, he advised, occurred no matter how clearly the issue in question appeared regulated by the contract. Such disputes were especially likely where the owner 'forces' a nominated subcontractor upon a general contractor. His words were to prove prophetic. Nevertheless, in spite of such reservations, Moreland came down in favour of appointing the steel subcontractor directly on the cost and schedule grounds mentioned above. The owner accepted this advice.

Another subcontract awarded directly by the owner was for the piling work. This had been awarded and work was underway by the time of my arrival on the scene in August 2000. The experience of awarding the piling contract left a lasting impression on the Moreland project management team, one that was to influence their views on the handling of subsequent tenders. To appreciate why, we need to briefly survey how tendering is regulated within the People's Republic.

A new tendering law, designed to cut down on corrupt practices, came into operation on the first day of 2000. To avoid underhand influence, detailed requirements are set out for each stage of the tendering process. To ensure compliance, a local construction tender office plays an active role in monitoring and validating each stage of the process. This, as was intended, removes control over the process from the owners and is intended to ensure that the bid is awarded according to criteria deemed fair by the tender office. While the aim is laudable, the result, from the point of view of the owner, can be lamentable. Regulatory bureaux are prone to take a more leisurely pace than those subject to them would wish the world over, and China is no exception. Matters are made worse, however, by the considerable freedom enjoyed by regulatory agencies in China in the interpretation of rules and regulations. Often these are phrased in general terms that demand interpretation, but even where they are quite explicit, exceptions are so frequently negotiable as to be expected. This, however, regularly requires a great deal of time and attention paid to currying favour. As far as the tendering for the piling was concerned, the project management team found that, instead of being a routine, it required their constant attention to the whims of the tendering officer in charge. There was also little faith in the work of the panel of experts appointed by the bureau to evaluate the tenders. While chosen at random they appeared to the Moreland technical manager to be chosen without reference to their expertise in the particular area in question and appeared to pay only cursory attention to detail.

This led to a desire to have as little to do with the tender office as possible. Fortunately, there did appear to be a way out. Foreign funded projects in the city were still being allowed, in some instances, to use a form of tendering known as 'negotiated tendering' under which the process was largely removed from the detailed supervision of the tender office, allowing far greater freedom to the owner to negotiate.

It appeared, however, that with exactly half the ownership of the enterprise resting with a Chinese government-sponsored body, that this might not be possible without direct lobbying of the local political leadership. With this in mind, members of the German board voiced their worries to the deputy mayor, who ordered that an exception should by made for the project and that they should be allowed to use negotiated tendering for the appointment of the general contractor. The joint venture was happy to secure the greater freedom that this allowed. This was just the sort of freedom, however, that the new laws were designed to abrogate, given the opportunity for distortions introduced by kickbacks and pull. As we shall see, suspicions were rife that this is just what was to happen within the project.

Some flavour of what was to be involved can be gathered by stepping forward some months to the opening of bidding for the landscaping. The two sides of the project management team, Moreland and the Land Development Corporation representatives, decided that each should put forward two companies for consideration, keeping the number to be considered within reasonable limits. It transpired that Martin Li, from Moreland, and Ma Bo, from the Land Development Corporation, had both recommended the same firm as one of their choices. Martin Li said that was excellent, as now they only had to consider three candidates. Ma Bo, however, insisted on being allowed to add another to his two choices to make up four. The deputy general manager, Zhang Haiying, then got to hear of the bidding and told the office staff to add two of her own recommendations to the list. This brought the number to six. The bidding list had to be registered with the municipal tender office, which in turn wanted to recommend the addition of one more candidate, a subsidiary, to the list, bringing the total to seven. This added to the time and effort needed by the process without any apparent compensation other than increasing the likelihood that the patron of the successful bidder would be able to claim some credit for its success.

Comparing the companies recommended for consideration for the general contractor and major subcontracts, while the Moreland side of the project management team favoured foreign involvement, the Chinese side invariably put forward local Chinese firms. There is doubtless an element of familiarity here, the Chinese know more about local firms, while Moreland prefers firms operating according to procedures similar to its own, firms that 'speak the same language'. There was also a widespread view among the Chinese staff of the project management team that Western firms were less attractive as potential sources of commission. Chinese firms also benefited from their local connections, with government influence wielded in favour of local firms. In a situation where the local government continues to participate in the ownership of local construction firms, any general predisposition on its part towards local firms is naturally reinforced. Itself owned by the local authority, the Chinese partner in the joint venture might be expected to be sensitive to such concerns.

The state of play when I arrived on the scene in August 2000 was as follows. The piling had commenced and the steel subcontractor had been nominated. The contest for the steel subcontract had finished up as a choice between two bidders, Gang Tie Consortium and City Mechanical Construction (CMC), with the contract awarded going to the former. Explanations differed as to why Gang Tie was successful. On the side of the German partner, Moreland and the architect, it was explained as a straightforward technical matter. Prominent was the preference of the architect for Gang Tie's proposed construction method. The head of the Chinese project management team had favoured CMC, however, and only withdrew his opposition to Gang Tie under instructions from the chairman of the board of the joint venture, the appointee of the Land Development Corporation. This enforced change of heart was to have repercussions later as the project manager appeared to harbour a grudge against Gang Tie and at times took evident satisfaction in turning down its requests. The tension often led to heated discussions between the project manager and Gang Tie's leading manager on the project, a Mr Shen. After one of their shouting matches, I teased Shen about Ma not liking him. 'It is because I am not good looking,' he responded. 'Actually, Ma Bo has never liked us. During the review of the bids, he always voted against us.'

When I expressed surprise at his knowing this, given that the discussions were supposed to be secret, he responded with a laugh, adding 'no wall can resist a penetrating wind.' This hint at Gang Tie's access to inside intelligence would appear to fit with the complaints of a senior manager from within CMC that their every submission during the negotiations must have been made available to Gang Tie, as it was matched at almost every step. Sources within CMC also claimed that their defeat was due to Gang Tie bribing a prominent official on the Chinese side of the partnership with a payment of a million yuan, a payment seemingly large in itself but small in relation to the contract. Such claims are commonplace in the industry, although separating a case of sour grapes from a well-founded allegation usually proves, as here, to be impossible.

Views on what lay behind their success varied within the Gang Tie Consortium. Some attributed it straightforwardly to the technical superiority of their bid, their price having been higher. Others saw others factors at work, viewing the award of the contract as a quid pro quo orchestrated by the local authority for a variety of favours extracted previously from Gang Tie. Most directly related to the project was the purchase of twenty-four flats from the Land Development Corporation. A number of other contributions forced on members of the consortium were held to weigh in its favour. These included the relocation of Gang Tie's main office to the special zone, an unwanted inconvenience that removed the headquarters far from the location of their plant on the other side of the city. There was also the takeover of loss-making local steel firms; taking a partnership in a major infrastructure project, widely thought of as likely to prove unprofitable; and financial contributions towards the cost to the city of hosting an important international political meeting. Such extractions and assistance are a regular feature of relations between local authorities and state-owned enterprises throughout China. Non-compliance can lead to the stick of numerous administrative burdens. On the other hand, there is the carrot offered by the understanding that some indefinite recompense will eventually be made. This fits well with the general tenor of Chinese paternalism in which children are expected to do what they are told, however onerous, on the implicit understanding that a benevolent parent will note their sacrifices and make amends at some unspecified future date. The manner in which Chinese organizational life is influenced by models drawn from family life is a topic to which we shall return in the next chapter.

Choosing the general contractor: the contenders

By the time of my arrival in August 2000 there were two contenders left in the race for appointment as the general contractor. One was a consortium composed of the local construction arm of a Korean conglomerate, Korean Construction, and a state-owned enterprise, City Number 11 Construction Company. The other was another consortium composed of a Hong Kong firm, HK Building, and another state-owned enterprise, City Construction Group (CCG).

As its name suggests, Number 11 Construction dates its origin back in the days of a command economy that had a prosaic preference for distinguishing work units by straightforward enumeration. However, compared with many other state enterprises it has managed the transformations of the reform period more successfully. It is recognized within the industry as more competent than many of its rivals and in possession of a healthier balance sheet.

During the command economy era before 1979 state-owned construction companies in the city, as elsewhere, were divided from one another in terms of the area allotted to them. Number 11 was fortunate in having the central region of the city. This is where most of the large building projects took place and provided the enterprise with a better income and wider experience than was available to its rivals. The various state construction companies in the city, Number 1, Number 2, and so on, have been freed from this anchorage in a particular district by the reforms and can now compete for contracts. Given its experience and resources, Number 11 was well placed in such competition. However in 2000, the construction industry, along with many others, was suffering from a depression that set in following the boom years earlier in the 1990s. While the state-owned construction enterprises were unlikely to face closure as a result, managers and staff of those with an empty order book could expect minimal wages. Number 11 was facing the same difficulty as its competitors in finding orders and was therefore keen to secure the contract for the exhibition centre. The lack of orders was also being felt by its Korean partner and its competitors, HK Building and CCG, and was to shape the concessions all were prepared to make in order to win the contract.

However, neither Number 11 nor CCG, the two local firms, could succeed on their own. An international element was necessary to calm the fears of the German partner and the architect about the competence of Chinese construction companies to handle the innovatory design and to communicate with the architect and owner effectively. In the case of Number 11, this meant establishing an alliance with the Korean conglomerate.

The Korean conglomerate had gained a toehold in the market when it was invited to construct the city's first elevated highway in the early 1990s, a time when Chinese construction firms lacked any experience in this area. Once Chinese contractors had learned the skill from this experience, however, the Korean firm found it received no further orders in this field. Its work was confined to projects invested in by its parent company and from other foreign firms familiar with its work overseas. Prominent here was the construction of one of the tallest buildings in Malaysia. By teaming up with Number 11, it hoped to break through what it saw as discrimination against non-Chinese construction firms.

As for its rival, CCG sought to secure the necessary international element through drawing in HK Building, which had involvement in the building of the new Hong Kong airport to its credit. HK Building had become involved in projects on the mainland through investing in the development of Hainan before progress on the island began to stall. Its willingness to become involved in that state-sponsored development project was nevertheless generally thought to have improved its ability to win other government contracts.

CCG emerged from what had been the City Construction Bureau. Before restructuring in the early 1990s the construction industry in the city operated within a system inherited from the days of the command economy. As is illustrated in Figure 4.1, the City Construction Bureau was subject to the dual control of the centre and the locality, with the vertical line of command leading down from the ministry carrying somewhat more weight. The City Construction Bureau had directly under its wing a number of central units and a series of localized construction units spread throughout the city. Elements of dual control continued down into the localities, with districts and counties playing a part in the running of the local units.

The reforms transformed the bulk of the City Construction Bureau into the City Construction Group, leaving behind a much smaller City Construction Committee charged with regulatory functions (see Figure 4.2). With the change, CCG itself was cut loose from its vertical ties to the ministry and was placed firmly under the leadership of the municipal government. It now functions as a holding company for the assets of the former City Construction Bureau. Part of its finances comes from remittances from the subsidiaries it has inherited, part from operating as a contractor on its own account.

As mentioned earlier, the formerly localized units of the bureau were cut loose from their local ties and now compete with one another for

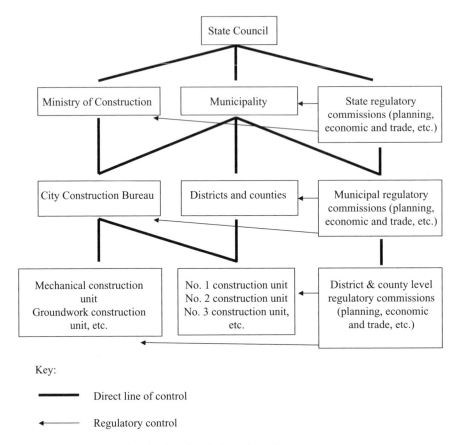

Figure 4.1 Construction in the city: before the reform

contracts. Each consists of a core and non-core element, the core containing the most profitable parts of each enterprise. Both core and non-core continue to work as one unit, sharing the same management and premises. The principal reason for the division was to gather the most appealing aspects of each under the umbrella of the City Construction Company to enable it to list successfully. As with other state enterprises, however, a majority shareholding remains with the state, allowing layers of coordination and dependence not allowed for in prospectuses to continue much as before.

This brings us back to the position of Number 11 Construction Company, which, as can be seen, is a subsidiary of its competitor for the project, CCG. Technically, there is nothing to prevent this: Number 11 simply has a duty to remit a negotiated amount of its profits to CCG and is free to vie for contracts as it pleases. Its freedom to do so is enhanced by its

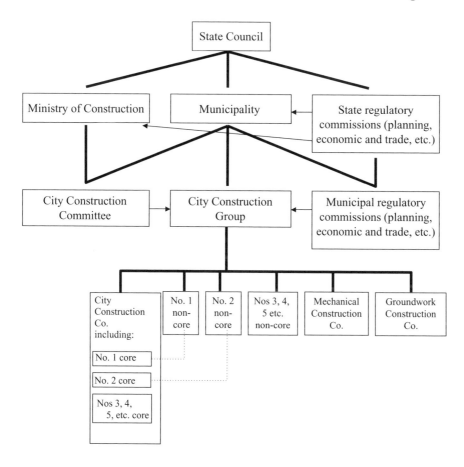

Key:

━━━━━━━ Direct line of control

◄━━━━━━ Regulatory control

⋯⋯⋯⋯⋯ Core and non-core share the same management and operation facilities. Core and non-core support each other in various ways

Figure 4.2 Construction in the city: after the reform

financial strength and the independence it accrued under the reform before the transformation of the City Construction Bureau into a holding company. Finding itself in competition for a project with CCG was not a novel occurrence. Nevertheless, such freedom as it enjoyed was not absolute. It appeared, like so much else, to be negotiable.

Post-tender review

The initial bids from the prospective general contractors had been received at the end of July and on my arrival in August meetings were taking place to examine the content of the two proposals in terms of cost, quality and completion dates. The initial proposal from Korean Construction/ Number 11 was for $52,883,133, giving it an advantage over the bid from HK Building/CCG, which stood at $59,451,807. The latter, however, fared better in terms of completion, with construction promised within 345 days in comparison with the 407 days on offer from Korean Construction/ Number 11. A third contender, a German-led consortium took part in the initial bid, with a price slightly below that of HK Building/CCG, but with a construction period that was several weeks longer than Korean Construction/Number 11. It withdrew, leaving the German side facing a choice between contractors unfamiliar to them. Following an initial round of discussions, revised bids were received on 15 August. HK Building/CCG reduced its price to $55,759.334. Korean Construction/Number 11 offered two prices, one higher than before at $53,246,988, the other lower at $51,513,555 in the event of being allowed to use some local products in place of the imported ones specified in the tender documents.

A difference between the joint venture partners concerning the two contenders was soon evident, with the Chinese side coming down on the side of HK Building/CCG. The Germans, on the other hand, were more disposed to favour Korean Construction/Number 11. Moreland supported them in this. The Chinese side of the project management team supported the Chinese preference. Thus the split in the project management mirrored that between the owners, leaving it unable to operate as a unified independent adviser.

It was clear that Moreland and its German sponsors had greater trust in the competence of Korean Construction/Number 11 and their ability to deliver on their promises. To a certain extent, their feeling more comfortable in communicating with each other inspired this. In negotiations, Korean Construction spearheaded the bid, with Number 11 playing a supporting role in the presentation of their proposals. Korean Construction's presentation was in marked contrast to that employed by their competitor and far more in accord with the international practices to which the Germans representatives and Moreland would be accustomed outside China.

The purpose of the post-tender review was to reassure the owners that the bidders had the capacity to carry out the work and to secure additional undertakings. The team from Korean Construction appeared businesslike and alert, turned out in suit and tie. It had clearly done its homework, arriving with an impressive PowerPoint presentation delivered succinctly in fluent English with simultaneous translation into Chinese by an interpreter with a degree in construction. The team was composed of well-trained engineers conversant with the project and at ease in the technical language needed to discuss potential problems. Where requests were made that were regarded as not technically feasible, this was simply stated. The tone of delivery was polite and composed. The prospective construction manager led the team, with additional members brought into the discussion as questions touched upon their area of expertise. The regional director of Korean Construction was part of the team, but his position was not announced until a question concerning the backing the team would receive from the office of the Korean firm came up, when he made mention of his position for the first time and pledged that backing would be provided.

The local partner, CCG, dominated the HK Building/CCG team. Its style of presentation and negotiation exhibited a point-by-point contrast with that just outlined for Korean Construction. The team was dressed casually and lacked the focused air of its competitor. It gave no presentation but arrived with a 'here we are, what do you want to ask us?' attitude. In early meetings, one of the team, a member of HK Building, spoke in English. At later meetings, he was not present and managers spoke directly in Chinese, leaving translation for the German participants to be provided by the client. The team had no specialists on hand ready to deal in technical terms with problems raised. There was, however, a boundless optimism expressed that whatever the problem might be, CCG could solve it. Far from being inscrutable, emotions were readily conveyed in tone of voice and non-verbal communication. Where Korean Construction simply stated its achievements, CCG announced its with expansive pride in its voice and gestures; whereas Korean Construction would meet an announcement by the owner that they could not yet decide on awarding the contract with a calm 'we understand your position,' CCG would clearly express its disappointment in tone and manner. The team did not involve anyone proposed to take a direct part in the work. The senior manager on the team was introduced at the beginning with great deference and similar attentiveness paid to displaying respect to the prominent Chinese members of the owners' party. Emphasis was laid on the connections enjoyed by CCG that would enable it to call up support from other parts of the state system.

One difference that weighed heavily against the Koreans from the point of view of Ma Bo, head of the project management team, was that the Korean managers could not speak Chinese, as Ma was unable to speak English. This in itself would clearly place him at a disadvantage in relation to Martin Li from Moreland in terms of his power to control the project. From the point of view of the Land Development Corporation in general, the manner of the Chinese team was also familiar, as familiar as Korean Construction's was to the German partner. Indeed, it was not only familiar, it was in certain respects superior, for it paid deference where deference was due and its claims to its connections within the state system placed it clearly within a world in which the Chinese were at home. Any failure to conform to Western business norms did not jar. It simply passed unnoticed.

The division over who should be awarded the contract found clear expression in a meeting held on 22 August. The Chinese side was composed of Wang Ke, chairman of the joint venture, Zhang Haiying, deputy general manager, Ma Bo, project manager, and Zhao Wenyan, interpreter. The German side was composed of four representatives from the three German exhibition firms constituting German Fair, most prominent of whom was Sprung, from Altdurf, who chaired the meeting. Martin Li of Moreland, deputy project manager, completed the team. My contribution was to take the minutes.

Sprung started the meeting by stating the German partner's preference for the Korean Construction/Number 11 bid and asking for the opinion of the Chinese partner. This was provided by Ma Bo, the project manager, who attacked Korean Construction as technically inferior to its competitor in terms of quality control, the materials to be used, construction methods and organization. He then mentioned the difference in building time before going on to cast doubt on Korean Construction's ability to provide items such as the roof at the low price it quoted. That it brought along its subcontractors to explain technical details relating to their area of responsibility was interestingly turned into evidence of weakness, an inability to grasp how things needed to be done in comparison with its competitors who fielded no such array of specialists.

In reply, Sprung stated that, despite Ma's observations, the German side regarded both bidders as equally competent, but that the price quoted by HK Building/CCG was over budget. As such, there was no possibility of giving it the contract, as the board had ordered that the budget should be adhered to strictly throughout. If, however, HK Building/CCG were to reduce their price, the German side would be prepared to consider it. At this point, the chairman of the board, Wang Ke, intervened to say that, while he agreed on the need to control spending, according to Martin Li's budget review, the bid from HK Building/CCG was within the budget. At this point he in turn was interrupted by Martin Li who dismissed Wang's comment by interjecting: 'Objection. He is calculating it wrongly.' Wang displayed clear annoyance at this, as well he might given its affront to the usual reluctance to openly contradict leaders characteristic of Chinese organizations. He nevertheless pressed on, stating that it was within budget if the contingency fund was devoted to filling the gap. It was to be hoped, nonetheless, that CCG could reduce its price, though not by too much as this might affect quality.

Opinions were exchanged on whether and when such a reduction might be expected, with Wang Ke insisting on the necessity of agreeing on an acceptable price before going further. Discussion then returned to the issue of Korean Construction, with Wang castigating them as being infamous for quoting unrealistically low prices. Martin Li responded by asking why the Chinese side had not objected to Korean Construction earlier. Ma Bo replied on their behalf that it was because they had expected Number 11 to be the leading partner, whereas now it was confined to a relatively minor role in taking care of the civil work. One of the German representatives remarked that they were still not convinced that Korean Construction could not do the job. Wang replied with evident annoyance: 'Then you insist on Korean Construction and we insist on CCG. Then the project will never begin.'

'But we are a joint venture,' Sprung protested, reacting to this intransigence. 'We need to find somewhere in the middle.' Martin Li reiterated that it was Moreland's professional opinion that Korean Construction/ Number 11 was best, but that they recognized that other considerations might play a part in the final decision. This failed to mollify Ma Bo, who dissociated the project management from Li's advice. Wang added to the attack, chastising Li for not being loyal to the project management and influencing the Germans in the wrong direction. Wang also complained that Martin Li had failed to send all his reports to him as chairman of the board of the joint venture, rather than to the German general manager of the joint venture in his capacity as the local representative of the German Fair company. Unruffled, Martin Li pointed out that under Moreland's contract he had no duty to report to the chairman. At this point Wang abruptly ended the meeting: 'I don't want to talk about this any more. Everyone has expressed his ideas. We go to have dinner.'

I, however, went off to an interview arranged with a contact in the construction industry in the city. The meeting had thrown the Chinese side into a more assertive and intransigent role than the Germans, who appeared open to persuasion and ready to stress how both sides needed to meet in the middle for the sake of the joint venture. The Chinese partners at times were openly angry and confrontational, with the Chinese chairman of the joint venture shouting and sulking. The Germans, in contrast, remained calm throughout and stressed the need to arrive at a compromise. This was the reverse of what might be expected from notions that the Chinese prefer more accommodating styles of conflict resolution. As mentioned earlier in discussing the work of Thomas, experience suggests that strong interests might well counterbalance any such preference. I wanted to try to get a better idea as to what interests lay behind the Chinese position.

My contact was Huang Xi, the owner of a private construction company that nevertheless gained most of its work as subcontractor to a state-owned enterprise, City Mechanical Construction (CMC), yet another subsidiary of CCG. I arrived late for our appointment, as the meeting had gone on for longer than expected because of the dispute. I explained this in apologizing to Mr Huang. He reacted with surprise:

Why are they wasting so much time and trouble on that? Everybody in the industry knows the work will go to CCG. All the major projects in city are done by CCG: the airport, the stadium, the city's tallest building. The city government would never give such a large project to an outside firm like Korean Construction. The city is running out of big projects this year. The local state-owned construction firms are running out of money. They are only managing to pay their workers a minimum basic salary and cannot pay off their debts to subcontractors. Even if CCG were not short of business, giving the job to Korean Construction would make them lose face.

The implication was that, whether by a wink and a nod or a straightforward command, the municipal government had instructed the Chinese side of the joint venture to secure the contract for HK Building/CCG. I was never able to gather firm evidence that such influence had indeed been brought to bear, but much circumstantial evidence accumulated in support of such an interpretation as events unfolded. It was also taken for granted by those inside the industry and familiar with its mode of operation that this would happen as a matter of course. It is also consistent with evidence from across China of the strength of local protectionism. In the city itself evidence of this daily confronts one on the streets. Local taxi ranks are made up exclusively of a locally produced joint venture sedan, the local government ensuring its monopoly through a mix of fiat and tailoring local regulations to exclude the possibility of competition from firms located elsewhere in China.

When I mentioned the next day to Martin Li, Moreland's project manager, that although the joint venture was busy arguing over which contractor to use, people in the local construction industry seemed to know in advance that HK Building/CCG were going to get the contract, the news came as no surprise. 'Yes, I know,' he replied. 'This is all politics, it is terrible.' However, not all the Moreland project management team seemed equally aware of the rumours. Lan Shoudong, the civil engineer, was surprised. As the civil engineer, he viewed his remit as confined to technical matters and simply wished that a decision were made speedily so that work could commence. Members of the commercial department, operating as part of the Chinese project management team, were also aware of the stand taken by the Chinese owners and were not happy with it as they felt it made something of a charade of all the time they had spent calculating costs and comparing bids. They also favoured the Korean Construction bid as commercially more sound and the company likely to be less trouble to administer as a general contractor than its rival, which they feared would be forever pressing them to make concessions.

The Germans, for their part, refused to treat the matter as settled. Neither did Korean Construction. When the commercial department rang HK Building/CCG to arrange a further post-tender meeting to discuss lowering the price as agreed at the previous day's meeting, ten minutes later Korean Construction/Number 11 was on the line. They said that they had heard that their rival had been invited for a review and wished to know when a similar review would be offered to them. Clearly, Korean Construction/

Number 11 had an informant within the ranks of their rival or those of the joint venture. In this, however, they were not alone, as their rivals also appeared to have an inside informant working on their own behalf, as we shall see.

A brief meeting with HK Building/CCG took place later that day, at which they submitted a reduced price, cutting their earlier figure by $900,000. At $54,863,078, this brought them to just below the joint enterprise budget for the general contractor. It still left them above either of the two alternative bids submitted by Korean Construction. Speaking for German Fair, one of the German representatives politely thanked HK Building/CCG, saying: 'We appreciate your work and we think you are competent technically, but we still require the price to be lower.' The German managers were very cool, but the Chinese chairman of the board of the joint venture was clearly furious and did not try to hide this. He openly told the bidder that he was unhappy that their reduced offer had not been accepted. 'Price is important, but not the most important issue,' he fumed. A meeting, he added, would be held to bring the Germans round. All this was translated. It led to some sideways glances among the Germans, but no open protest as throughout the Germans showed reluctance to openly air divisions with their Chinese partner in negotiations with outsiders. This was not the case with the Chinese partner, which was clearly more interested in supporting the bidder than in preserving a united front as a joint venture. This was given visible expression at meetings in seating arrangements. Up to this point, the Chinese partner's team had sat together with their German partner and the Moreland team facing the bidders as a group across the table. The next day a further meeting took place with HK Building/CCG. This found the Chinese team of the joint venture sitting together with HK Building/CCG, facing their German partners and Moreland from the other side of the table. It was an arrangement that was to last throughout the remainder of the negotiations.

For their part, relations within the HK Building/CCG team had undergone a change. Previously active in presentations, the Hong Kong side was from now on to play a passive role, remaining completely silent with CCG doing the talking. This appeared to mark a recognition that the matter had now shifted from a competition judged purely on commercial grounds to one that was to stress the official backing enjoyed by CCG. This was apparent from the moment the meeting at which the reduced price was offered commenced. The CCG leader started his address to the client with 'Dear leaders, ladies and gentlemen,' clearly conveying the impression that the relationship between CCG and the Chinese client was less that of independent contractor and commercial client than that of a government authority dealing with a state-owned enterprise. On its own, of course, this phrasing may simply have been a slip of the tongue, revealing though this may be. However, it did fit entirely with the manner in which the Chinese side of the joint venture put itself out to lead and assist HK Building/CCG in the discussions, even to the extent of arranging for them to have a German interpreter. CCG was also keen to stress not only its loyalty to the government, but also that it could call upon government support. They could, the CCG vice-chairman claimed, 'have the government help shorten the construction period so that the September exhibition could be held.'

Despite all this, the German side pressed ahead with considering both bids. The next day, 24 August, a meeting was convened with Korean Construction/Number 11. On his way to the meeting, Steinhausen, the general manager of the joint venture bumped into Ma Bo, the Chinese project manager, and invited him to participate. Ma Bo refused, indicating once again the split in the project management team that mirrored the division within the joint venture and stopped the project management acting as an independent professional adviser to the joint venture as a whole. The Chinese side of the joint venture had by this time made clear their strong desire to confine negotiations to HK Building/CCG and refused to take part in further discussions with Korean Construction. German Fair insisted on continuing, however, and did so without the presence of their Chinese partner, but assisted by the Moreland element of the project management team. The negotiations were clearly not merely a ploy to put pressure on the other side as they mainly revolved around technical questions and how Korean Construction/Number 11 might be able to bring their completion date forward.

Nevertheless, there appears to have been some concern on the part of both CCG and their Chinese joint venture sponsors that the Germans were trying to entangle them in a downward spiral of competitive bidding with Korean Construction. This was revealed in constant requests from both to the German side that an acceptable figure be settled upon. The suspicion may well have an element of projection in it, as the technique is one that Chinese negotiators have long employed against foreign firms. In discussing Chinese negotiating tactics of twenty years ago, for example, Pye recalls how commonly Chinese negotiators would house contending foreign bidders in the same hotel, moving back and forth between them to get each to continue undercutting the other (1982).

Continuing with their intention of allowing each side to have an equal say, Martin Li instructed the commercial department to invite HK Building/CCG to a meeting later in the day. Shortly after the call was placed, his Chinese counterpart, Ma Bo, appeared at the door of the department demanding: 'Who among you phoned CCG inviting them for a meeting here?' On being told that Martin Li had ordered it, he left, clearly fuming. This added to the impression of a breakdown in coordination within the project management and clearly indicating how CCG must have been on the phone to their established ally on the project management team to find out what was afoot the moment they received the invitation.

At the meeting, held later that day, both sides of the joint venture and project management attended. The German team asked HK Building/CCG whether they could reduce their price if they could construct just two of the halls in readiness for the September exhibition, leaving the other two until later. HK Building/CCG responded by saying that their quote had already taken this into account, as they proposed to complete just two of the halls inside and out by the September deadline, erecting just the shell of the other two. When the Germans said they were only interested for the moment in having the two finished in time without erecting the other two in any form until later, the bidder stated that this was impossible. To finish only two, they stated, would leave the two standing in a construction site and this would spoil their appearance. The Germans were clearly some- what taken aback at being told by a prospective contractor the number of halls they were to have and when they were to have them. In discussions with the Germans after the meeting it was clear that they were nonplussed as to why HK Building/CCG insisted on completing the structure of all four by September. In the absence of understanding, their bemusement served to fuel their distrust of HK Building/CCG.

I raised this question with an old acquaintance, the former general man- ager of City Mechanical Construction, the subsidiary of CCG, Mr Zhuang. Zhuang said that in all likelihood the municipal government had told CCG that they were not allowed to build two halls only. The problem was, he continued, that the Germans did not understand China. The city government would naturally like to have the halls finished in time for the September exhibition with the prospect of having Chancellor Schroeder attending. This would show how successful the city was in attracting foreign investment and serve to promote this further. Furthermore, if Premier Zhu Rongji also attended the opening, this would give a great deal of face to the local mayor. The Chinese client would in turn win praise and its leaders' careers would be enhanced. 'Two halls only will look less impressive for a picture in the newspaper or on TV,' he concluded. 'Zhu Rongji will come to see and will ask "Why so small?" So it is perfectly natural that the Chinese client wants the four halls ready. The Germans simply do not understand the Chinese situation.'

The meeting continued with the Germans pressing for a further reduction in the price on offer. At this, the deputy general manager of the joint venture, Zhang Haiying remarked in the local dialect to the CCG repre- sentatives: 'They just want you to give them the project for free. They are very mean about giving money to the contractor, but when they spend money on themselves they are very generous.' (There may have been an element of personal pique at work here, as a week earlier she was to be heard at lunch complaining bitterly to one and all of Steinhausen's refusal to spend money on a computer she had requested.)

Ma Bo, in his concluding speech, told the bidder, his voice heavy with sarcasm: 'Our client will not ask for an unreasonable price. Asking for an unreasonable price would not be mature. After all, our client has already paid six million dollars to Young and Muller, the architect. Six million dollars!' Zhang Haiying added, again out loud but again in the local dialect, which always escaped translation: 'That's true, they gave so much money to the Americans, but when they need to spend money on us Chinese they are so bloody mean and stubborn to boot.' At the end of the meeting, the head of CCG told Ma Bo: 'Our leaders are taking care of us so well, we will do the job very well.' This left Ma Bo smiling, looking quite the part of the revered patron.

At the conclusion of the round of meetings just described, the two competitors were asked to submit revised proposals by 10 a.m. on 28 August. However, on the morning of the deadline the commercial department received only one submission. This was from Korean Construction/Number 11. Shortly after its arrival, Ma Bo, the project manager, entered the office and, hearing of its arrival, ordered that it should be returned unopened. He left, to be followed shortly by Steinhausen, the general manager, asking after the bids. On being told of the arrival of the bid from Korean Construction/Number 11, he asked for it and took it off with him. Later Ma Bo came back and was clearly upset to hear that the bid had not been returned. He went to Steinhausen and protested that the bid should be returned as he had directed. Steinhausen refused, but said that he would keep the bid unopened for the time being. Ma Bo was not satisfied and went off to complain to the chairman of the board of the joint venture, Wang Ke. As a result, Wang wrote to the board stating that he felt the tendering was not being handled properly and that he was suspending the entire process by virtue of his position as chairman.

The state of deadlock this had thrown the tendering into was naturally the focus of the weekly project meeting that took place shortly after, on 30 August. Present were the general manager, Dr Steinhausen, the deputy general manager, Zhang Haiying, and Martin Li, the deputy project manager from Moreland. I was present to take the minutes. Martin Li opened the meeting by asking where the absent chairman, Wang Ke, was, to which Zhang Haiying replied in a scornful tone, 'Hiding.' Both she and Martin Li expressed the view that Steinhausen had the authority as general manager to receive the submission, providing he did not open the document on his own. Steinhausen was clearly relieved to secure confirmation that his action in accepting the tender had been in order and anxious to have this support recorded prominently in the minutes. The chairman's letter clearly expressed criticism of his having gone against the advice of Ma Bo on this issue. The letter was addressed to the board and Steinhausen was evidently worried that it might put his position at risk.

Zhang Haiying had also changed her tune from the previous meetings, where, it may be recalled, she was less than complimentary about the Germans. As I got to know her better it seemed to me that she was one more likely than most to tailor her opinions to fit with her audience, at times making it difficult to know what her real views were. She had gained her success through political skills that enabled her to rise in the local government. In China as elsewhere, the ability to appear all things to all people can prove an asset to a political career. Nevertheless, on this occasion she did seem genuinely worried that the joint venture was falling apart. For all her earlier barbed comments against the Germans, if they went with them would go her job, one that paid several times her previous salary. 'Has,' she enquired with a worried air, 'anybody among the partners and the directors stated that they wanted to scrap the whole project?'

The chairman, she felt, should not be hiding himself away. Conciliation not confrontation was called for. 'If there are any disputes, we should sit down and discuss and find ways to solve the problem rather than stop communication altogether. No matter whether it is Germans or Chinese, behaving like this is improper.'

Martin Li then raised the issue of whether the steel subcontract should be signed, given that the contract involved a large sum of money and that if the project fell to pieces then this would be wasted. With the two sides involved in such a serious dispute, perhaps it would be better not to sign. Both Steinhausen and Zhang Haiying felt that they should go ahead and sign, given that the board had already granted permission for them to do so. I should like to be able to report that this unusual meeting of minds was prefaced by a pregnant pause and a meaningful exchange of glances, but if it was then they eluded me. Nevertheless, the temptation to see it as in both their interest to commit the partners more closely to the project by making it costly for them to retreat was difficult to resist.

Perhaps catching the drift of the conversation, Martin Li changed tack, mentioning how Gang Tie was keen to celebrate the signing of the contract on a particularly auspicious day that was fast approaching and so they should perhaps sign the contract soon to accommodate them. (Many firms in China, even state firms, much prefer to mark the start of an important new venture by launching it on a day regarded as auspicious and will routinely consult feng shui masters to choose the best date.)

Martin Li then went on to suggest that there should be an emergency meeting of the board of directors to resolve the impasse:

> Such disputes will not happen again in the fifty-year history of the joint venture. Arguments over such a large amount of money will not happen again. When the exhibition centre is built, the joint venture partners will quarrel over how to make money rather than spending money.

Despite the convergence of interests revealed in the meeting, elsewhere the conflict still drove the two sides apart. At lunch a couple of days later Zhang Haiying was eating together with the chairman, Wang Ke, when Steinhausen came in. Formerly Wang Ke and Zhang Haiying, particularly Zhang Haiying, would draw him into conversation, chatting about Germany and what to the Chinese serves as a topic of perennial interest, food. Now, however, neither talked to Steinhausen. Neither side made eye contact to even acknowledge the other's existence. Dr Steinhausen sat with the German member of the Moreland project management and soon left.

The staff of the commercial department, who, as mentioned earlier, were disposed to favour Korean Construction, were taken aside and given a talking to, told to be loyal to the Chinese side of the joint venture and to have nothing to do with Korean Construction and not to discuss the tenders with others.

Given this general atmosphere of gloom surrounding the prospects for the joint venture, I was surprised to find that opinions on this issue held in the local construction community were far more sanguine. Mr Zhuang, the former head of the CCG subsidiary referred to earlier, said that the project was bound to go ahead. If things became worse, then the government would intervene. When I mentioned that time was passing and the completion target might not be met, Zhuang continued:

> It is a bit tight. But this is China. How many hours do the Americans and English work? Six hours, eight hours? Here we work twenty-four hours. We have lots of people, when the project needs to be finished we will have three shifts and the government will coordinate and get people from other companies to divide the work. It will be built for the exhibition.

Zhuang has a confidence and pride widespread in the city nowadays. Echoing the newspapers and the television there is the feeling that the Chinese in general and the local citizens in particular can achieve anything. If this or that is not possible overseas, it is possible in this city. Everyone is pleased to accept government claims about breaking records. There is a 'can-do' outlook that has had many positive benefits. Without it, the impressive skyline of the city would never have arisen. Nevertheless, everything has the defects of its qualities. Such optimism can easily lead firms to promise more than they find themselves capable of delivering, putting aside planning in the belief that whatever the bridge they will prove up to crossing it once they get there.

In the event, the warring parties withdrew from the brink and the tendering process restarted, with the two candidates invited to submit revised tenders. The government may indeed have had a hand in this, as at a meeting held on 8 September the chairman of the joint venture remarked that the local government realized what had been happening. The local government had been in discussion with the Chinese partner about it, expressing the hope that a compromise could be reached with HK Building/ CCG and that they would carry out the work. The tenders were received on 8 August, Korean Construction/Number 11 offering a price of $52,591,923 which left them still ahead of their rival which had cut its price to $53,902,315. The German partner was still unwilling to accept HK

Building/CCG on these terms. It was decided that one final bidding round would be allowed to settle the matter. The final bid was received on 13 September and opened in the presence of the municipal tendering office. Korean Construction/Number 11 had brought its price to $52,341,432, HK Construction/SCG to $52,320,889. The locally preferred candidate had finally won by a whisker.

The bids were submitted in Chinese currency and, taking into account some additional amounts for the provision of an outdoor exhibition area, the gap between the two bids was 100,000 yuan, with HK Building/CCG asking 437,900,000 yuan in comparison with Korean Construction/Number 11's bid set at 438,000,000 yuan. A difference so small and so exact inevitably excited comment, with speculation rife that the successful bidder had acquired inside knowledge of its competitor's bid. Whether justified or not in this particular case, there was a widespread feeling that such leaks were only to be expected. Number 11 was suspected by many of having yielded to pressure, but the head of the Korean Construction thought this was probably not the case.

On the question of leaks, the German engineer attached to the Moreland team claimed interested parties on the other side of town would know news of meetings and decisions taken within the joint venture within the minutes rather than hours. He thought that his work and home telephones were tapped, along with others involved in the project. This is a common belief among foreigners working in China, but it is impossible to judge where paranoia ends and justified suspicion begins. I recall asking someone who worked with the public security bureau as a translator whether the foreign teachers at my university were justified in their fears about phone tapping and being bugged. Reassuringly for them, if somewhat unflatteringly, I was told that the bureau thought them too far too insignificant, reserving its attention for foreigners involved in matters of more commercial interest.

Yet, one probably does not have to posit the intervention of full-time professional spies and the apparatus of the security services to explain the leaks. The construction industry in the city is a small world where everyone knows everyone else and the exchange of tips and favours are commonplace. Arranging tip-offs in such a situation would not be difficult. Even in the absence of such arrangements, gossip does not take long to get about.

Drawing up the contracts

Having opted for HK Building/CCG, the joint venture might have hoped its problems were at an end. However, a letter Martin Li wrote to the chairman of the board of the German Fair immediately after the decision was confirmed must have dashed any such hope. In the letter Martin Li pointed out that much remained to be clarified and negotiated with the contractor before a formal award notice was issued. The split within the project management had not been healed by the conclusion of the tendering: Martin Li was already facing resistance from his Land Development Corporation-appointed counterpart as project manager in seeking to bring more items against HK Building. That the split in attitude was likely to persist is clear from what Li wrote. He foresaw two problems in controlling the contractor on site: first, bringing quality up to standard; second, controlling cost. On the question of quality, he predicts a problem arising from Moreland not having the power to instruct the contractor to rectify work 'without another signature from the Land Development Corporation'. Here he clearly anticipates a gulf opening up between the Land Development Corporation and Moreland and German Fair over questions of quality. He also points out that Moreland would not have enough arms and legs on site to enable it to safeguard quality.

As mentioned, Martin Li also saw a further split opening within the project management over keeping costs within budget. As he was to comment in an email on 25 September to the designer of the air-handling units:

> We are appointing the local general contractor, which, in our opinion, will agree on any price beforehand to win the job. I have warned the Owner that we expect we will be called upon very often to use the contingency during the construction phase, whether the contract is incontestable or not.

A further split within the project management was expected from the Land Development Corporation side taking a more generous view than Martin Li. However, the need to secure Moreland's joint agreement to claims might restrain the other side. For claims there would inevitably be. To quote the email once again:

> The use of contingency will come in the form of variations for issues such as AHU [air-handling units] on which the contractor doesn't understand at tender stage your requirements and details as the result of using less experienced local contractor. That's why Moreland has all the way suggested a real international contractor such as Zublin to take up the job.

Clearly, HK Building was not viewed as a 'real' international contractor in the eyes of Moreland or else its role was seen as insufficient to make up for the perceived shortcomings of its local partner, CCG. To try to address this issue Martin Li added additional clauses to the contract making it quite explicit that the contractor had to agree with the tender specifications and architects requirements in fine detail with regard to the air-handling units. While he hopes this would give them final control, he clearly has his doubts. 'In any case,' he concludes, 'we have to sign the contract in order that the project can move.'

CCG was not unique in its attitude to the contract. This can be better understood when set against broader trends of which it is a part. There is, to begin with, a general tendency on the part of Chinese construction firms to pay less attention to providing detailed plans of what they are going to do and when and how they are going to do it. This frequently drew comment from those on the project familiar with construction practices outside China. During the piling work, the contract clearly states that detailed programmes had to be provided by the local subcontractor at each stage of the work. The subcontractor did not see the importance of such a programme and provided a general outline with little relevance to the specific work to be undertaken. The subcontractor had to be persuaded about the importance of the programme and was asked to revise the programme three times. Finally, it looked acceptable, but when work commenced the programme was not followed. For the piling company, the programme was seen as nothing but a document that the foreigners stubbornly insisted upon. More generally, it was acknowledged by the Moreland team that some Chinese firms had acquired the ability to turn out impressive programmes; with the caveat that these were frequently set aside once the work was in progress. Embedding such programmes in the contract could not be relied upon to rein in such cavalier behaviour.

This doubtless owes much to the different attitudes towards contract between China and the West. The Chinese attitude towards the contract leans more towards the view that it is not the final word, but an important summation of negotiations to date, negotiations that can be expected to continue into the future. As a result contracts tend to be brief and will often serve to confirm cooperation that has already commenced rather than acting as the means to initiate it. A mixture of traditional Chinese values and state ownership is at work here, both bolstering a preference for arriving at mutual agreement over legal confrontation. Among Chinese firms, most contracts tend to be short, leaving much to be settled based on 'mutual understanding and trust', rather than attempting to encapsulate all major eventualities in explicit legal language.

The case of the steel subcontractor illustrates this. The Gang Tie Consortium was made up of three firms, all linked ultimately to Gang Tie Steel Group, two as subsidiaries, one direct, one distant, and a long-term business associate. These came together specifically to bid for the exhibition centre contract. The consortium itself was not initially bound by a contract and one was only drawn up among them on the insistence of the joint venture. It was just one page long, setting out their relationship in the most general terms and allotting overall guidance of the consortium to one of its number. The joint venture expressed its dissatisfaction with this choice and asked for one of the other members to be given this responsibility. The consortium readily obliged, simply adding on a sentence stating that general charge was given to the preferred company. In doing so, it failed to strike out the earlier nomination, leaving the situation hopelessly confused. I must admit to finding such a careless attitude towards the contract difficult to understand when I first encountered it. However, as work on the project progressed, the scepticism about the value of spending much time and thought on attempting to govern the distribution of authority by contract took on a new light.

The translation of the contract between the joint venture and the steel subcontractor into Chinese was very poor, despite having being entrusted to a leading foreign languages university. Paragraphs had been left out and clauses frequently mistranslated. One stating that the subcontractor was to obtain an insurance policy to cover their office building on site, for example, was mistranslated as the subcontractor had to ensure that the building was safe. Clearly, even in a university setting, the importance of the need for close attention to the meaning of a contract was not fully appreciated. Members of the commercial department assigned the task of improving the translation took an equally easygoing approach, satisfied with a loose translation or one that appeared probably correct. The project manager appointed by the Chinese partner, Ma Bo, brooded over the clauses beginning 'in the event of', worrying that detailed mention of hypo-thetical and undesirable events might tempt fate, again focusing on the contract as a symbolic expression of intent, though here of the bad variety.

While a difference between the current Chinese approach to contracts and that familiar to the West needs to be recognized, Chinese firms are not indifferent to every aspect of the contracts they sign. They pay partic-ular attention to whether a firm has the legal right to undertake the work it agrees to and whether the signatory has the authority to sign. Evidence is also expected of bank performance bonds. Setting the price and comple-tion date is fought over. Even though CCG was prepared to agree almost any price to win the contract in the hope that it could make additional claims during the course of construction, it still strove to get the highest price it could incorporated in the contract.

Where the difference mainly lay was in the detail, a point reflected in the burgeoning length of contracts in the West. Even there, however, there is a limit. One cannot devise written rules to cover every eventuality. The result is that written contracts are inevitably incomplete and need to be supple-mented by understandings and arrangements that help align the interests of the various parties. Nor has the shape and role of contracts outside China remained constant. During the course of my fieldwork, I interviewed the head of the leading British construction consultancy in the city. Comparing his experience of the construction industry in China and Britain, he remarked that before the wave of privatization, construction deals in Britain did not have to use lawyers and contracts all the time. As he remarked:

> It was much the case of a handshake; the deal is done. The finance bit could be left for the financial department to sort out later on. Business was easy. With most of the infrastructure construction being

state owned, the owner did not worry too much about money. But now everything is privatized and competition in the construction industry is tough, and doing anything has to go through complex and slow procedures with seeing lawyers, banks. In China, deals are still done by a handshake; details can be sorted out later. Such trust built from good relationships makes business deals much quicker and easier. Mind you, establishing the relationship in the first place does take time and effort. I end up taking lots of people back to visit England. Even their kids.

Within China, too, new attitudes towards contracts are emerging, with gaps opening between the generations in consequence, as can be seen when the day for signing the steel subcontract finally arrived. I had been asked to proofread the contract. On arrival, the steel company team was presented with the revised version.

The older managers asked whether there had been any changes from the draft sent to them a few days earlier. On being informed that there were only a few minor spelling corrections they said that they were happy with that and ready to sign. However, the younger managers objected. They dragged their elders aside, warning them against the possibility of the purchaser having changed the terms of the contract. While other old managers ignored this and prepared to sign, one older manager attempted to reassure the younger ones: 'Don't worry, if they put some extra work in, we simply won't do it.' The younger ones insisted: 'But if we don't do it, they can take us to the court and sue us for a lot of money.' The older managers laughed. One said: 'But we are all from the same locality, we all know each other. After all, business is based on trust.' Somewhat surprisingly, the younger ones still insisted and the older managers decided to compromise. They asked me to point out the pages that had been revised for their young colleagues to check for any changes of significance. The younger managers then went over the pages very carefully while their older colleagues sat back smoking and chatting.

For all that, it should not be assumed that the Gang Tie Group were happy with the contract they had signed with the client. Later in private conversation, they were to grumble to me about the unfair conditions they felt they had been forced to accept. They had signed because they needed the contract. They had not signed, however, with a feeling of 'that is the best we could get and now we are going to have to do it.' Rather it was an attitude of 'we have asked for the unreasonable conditions to be changed. The other side has been unreasonable in refusing. Therefore it is only to be expected that we should not feel obliged to carry out such an unreasonable request should circumstances allow.'

When it came to drawing up the contract for the general contractor, this was to incorporate features threatening the possibility of future clashes. The preparation of the translation of the final version into Chinese was entrusted to a member of the commercial department. This was later amended by the head of the department, who drew upon a Chinese version of a standard international construction contract to copy entire clauses. When the original translator pointed out this would not match any alterations introduced by the Moreland commercial adviser, she pressed on regardless.

The failure of the two to match would not be important if the English version were to have priority. This, however, soon became a cause of disagreement. The question of which language was to have priority first raised its head when the local office with authority over this matter insisted that the arbitration clause in the contract should specify Chinese as the language to be used in the event of arbitration. Clearly, they did not know or chose to ignore that the Chinese International Economic and Trade Arbitration Commission does allow English as the language of arbitration. Nevertheless, it was decided to change the clause to specify that arbitrators should speak both Chinese and English fluently. I pointed out to Martin Li that this was likely to exclude foreign arbitrators and that this might disadvantage the German side. However, Li dismissed this, saying that if things ever deteriorated to the extent that arbitration was called upon, the project would have fallen beyond all hope of salvation, a sentiment widely shared in the project.

The bureau then expanded its demands concerning the place to be accorded to Chinese. The contract held that the Chinese version and the English version were to have equal status, but that in the case of any discrepancy in technical specifications, the English version was to prevail. An official from the bureau telephoned the project to complain that the part of the clause relating to technical discrepancies was insulting to the Chinese and the Chinese contractors. When it was pointed out that all the technical documents were in English and that translation would pose great difficulties, the official was further incensed rather than mollified, shouting that this further insulted the ability of Chinese translators. Martin Li was unfailingly polite, but clearly exasperated by this, eventually instructing that the official was to be told he was out whenever he telephoned in the future.

His place in the fray was taken by the general manager and deputy general manager, who went to visit the office to persuade it to drop its objection on this point. The negotiations, however, failed to reach agreement. According to the person in charge of dealing with the regulatory bodies, the whole affair had been instigated by the Chinese project manager, Ma Bo, who had telephoned the bureau to bring the matter to its attention. If this were indeed the case, then he may well have been motivated by his struggle with Martin Li over control of the project management, the latter's command of English putting him at an advantage while so much of the contract remained in English.

HK Building/CCG also joined in the argument, adding their voice to that of the bureau, suggesting that the contract should be rendered entirely into Chinese and that Chinese should have priority throughout. It was widely assumed that here they were playing for time, for a clause in the contract meant that the longer it took the project management to secure the necessary construction permits, dependent on the signing of the contract, the more days they would have in which to complete the construction.

The disagreement dragged on with no sign of resolution. Then, quite suddenly, the objections ceased and the contract was signed. In terms of settling disputes, a new factor had evidently entered into the equation. Its emergence on to the scene marks a new stage in the project and its introduction awaits the next chapter.

5 Foundations

The previous chapter ended with the sudden resolution of a number of problems that had been holding up completion of the contract. This unexpected turn of events arose through the intervention of one of the deputy mayors. At first sight, he appeared to have suddenly taken it into his head to take a personal interest in the project. In retrospect, however, his interest might well have been anticipated, for it was rooted in the 'key project' status of the exhibition centre.

That the project enjoyed this standing was in itself the result of a misunderstanding. The German partners had heard mention of such a status, and, without fully appreciating all its implications, had pressed their Chinese partners to secure it. In their mind's eye recognition as a key project was largely a matter of status and as such would be good for publicity. The Chinese partner was also happy with the idea, though in their case it was because involvement in a key project held out the hope of rapid promotion. The municipal authorities were pleased, as key projects are chosen in part for their value in highlighting the achievements in office of the local cadres. Usually key projects are funded from the public purse, but here was the opportunity to gain a key project to add to their list of achievements at little direct cost. Everyone seemed happy. When the deputy mayor intervened on his own initiative to move things along, this appeared to be an added bonus to the German partners. Little did they foresee the darker side of the mayor deciding to take a hand.

The responsibility for key projects at the city level is divided among the deputy mayors, each being given responsibility for a certain number. Going through his portfolio one day, the mayor responsible for the exhibition centre decided to telephone Zhang Haiying, the deputy general manager, to find out how matters were progressing. When she explained the delays facing the project in terms of securing official permits and the signing of the contract, he instructed her to telephone the various agencies involved to tell them that he wished the permits to be issued without further delay.

After a round of telephone calls the deputy general manager appeared in the commercial department, evidently well pleased with herself, and issued instructions for the building permit to be collected from the construction bureau. This caused some surprise, as the permit should not be issued until the contract is signed. Nevertheless, given that construction had already commenced despite not having received the various necessary official permissions to proceed, it seemed much in accord with the general upside-down manner in which official permissions and performance were related throughout the project. As for the contract itself, the bureau was persuaded to drop its objections relating to the use of English. It also seems likely that the feelings of the deputy mayor were made known to CCG, as their foot-dragging over the contract ceased and it was signed shortly after, their reservations forgotten.

Yet, all was far from plain sailing from then on. The general contractor appointed was turning out to have a quite different character from that expected.

HK Building

Some hint of what was to come arose immediately following the initial award of the contract. Overnight the attitude of the general contractor began to change. It began to take on a less respectful and accommodating attitude toward the owner and the project management. It is, of course, unsurprising that some such slippage should occur. Applicants the world over are on their best behaviour. More surprising, however, was that the general contractor turned out to have an identity different from that anti-cipated. The HK Building arm of the general contractor joint venture had, as mentioned in the previous chapter, moved into a back-seat role during the course of the bidding process. Technically, however, it remained in overall control, with a 51 per cent shareholding. It might have been expected to move back into the driving seat once the contract was awarded, given its majority shareholding and its technical superiority. It was clearly hoped by the German side that its participation and leadership would move construction quality towards acceptable international standards required by the complexity of the design.

It was, then, to the HK Building managers that the owner at first addressed complaints about the failure of the general contractor to co-ordinate subcontractors. The HK Building managers seemed the natural target due to their greater familiarity with international standards and modes of operation, quite apart from their position as majority shareholder in the general contractor. Despite renewing their efforts in response to complaints from the owner, the HK Building managers found themselves unable to exercise authority over the subcontractors. As one replied in response to criticism from the architect about the performance of the subcontractors, 'I have told these guys to do it in this way, but they won't listen.' Sub-contractors nominated by HK Building's CCG partner would frequently ignore instructions from the HK Building managers. Far from siding with their Hong Kong partner, CCG appeared happy to let the subcontractors listen only to the CCG side, undermining the authority of the HK Building managers.

The HK Building managers were acutely aware of being caught in the middle of the division between the Chinese and German side of the joint venture that permeated the project. To a further request from the architect, which under the terms of the contract should have been sufficient, the HK Building manager just quoted replied: 'I am willing to agree with you, but this is a joint venture, I have to discuss this with the Chinese side.'

Speaking to me, the leader of the HK Building team said: 'I am supposed to be number one, but nobody listens to me.' By the end of November, the de facto position was recognized de jure, with the CCG share replacing HK Building as the 51 per cent shareholder in their joint enterprise. Having had the price forced down at the bidding stage, HK Building was unable to bring in enough personnel from Hong Kong to remain in control of the general contractor work given the resistance they faced and the salaries expected by Hong Kong personnel. Those that remained were increasingly sidelined. Despite this, the title of general manager of the general contractor continued to remain with the head of the HK Building team throughout the project. In reality, however, power rested throughout with the deputy general manager, the head of the CCG team. By February, the general manager was gloomily admitting this, protesting when addressed by his title: 'Don't call me general manager, I am not general manager anymore.'

The position of the HK Building managers is interesting because it went against a general trend within the project for Chinese participants to view their relations with their foreign collaborators very much in terms of 'us and them'. The Hong Kong managers tended to be more even-handed in their approach, siding sometimes with the Chinese side, sometimes with the Germans according to their professional judgement. In general, however, this meant that they were more often on the side of the Germans than the Chinese. This was a matter partly of shared standards, with the standards of the Hong Kong managers having more in common with the foreign participants on the project than the mainland Chinese managers in matters such as quality and safety. This encouraged a sense of professional fellow feeling that united the Hong Kong managers and the Western experts participating in the project that appeared stronger than any national sentiments binding them to their mainland compatriots. This lack of ethnic solidarity with their mainland compatriots and a feeling of affinity with the foreigners was doubtless also enhanced by both feeling themselves to be in a country that appeared happy to ignore their standards and talents.

The fate of the Hong Kong manager in charge of mechanical and electrical installation illustrates this. Unlike the mainlanders on the project, his relationships with the German technical consultants to the owner were close, cordiality building upon their shared professional interests and standards. This closeness, however, instead of being regarded as an asset by the dominant CCG side of the general contractor, was regarded as a weakness, as consorting with the enemy. Indeed, the manager in question was very open in his expression of outrage at subcontractors for their failure to meet required quality standards and the use of inferior products in place of those stipulated in the contract. He would come to the commercial department of the project management, pointedly shut the door, and recount to everybody the latest failure of the subcontractors to meet agreed standards. He could expect a sympathetic audience from the commercial department, most of its staff having been trained in Hong Kong on secondment.

Unfortunately, shutting the door was not enough to stop word spreading of what was seen by the mainland side of the general contractor as the Hong Kong manager's 'disloyalty'. He was ordered to have no further contact with the architect and foreign technical advisers to the owner. They, in turn, were told that any communication through the manager would not be accepted. Kept on, he was nevertheless isolated and his views overridden by the CCG managers of the general contractor.

The neutralization of HK Building rested on a number of factors. CCG was, as we shall see, under pressures that led to issues of quality being downplayed, with a willingness to let subcontractors cut corners. This laxity was further encouraged in the case of those subcontractors that were themselves subsidiaries of CCG. Yet, there was also the difficulty that the standards with which HK Building was familiar were quite unfamiliar to the local contractors. As the general manager remarked:

> It is very difficult for me to manage, the subcontractors are simply not qualified. They will not understand what I am asking for because they have a much lower standard. Also, because they have never seen what is of a good standard, they think they are the world's best. They are not prepared to seek any advice.

HK Building's own experience elsewhere in China showed, however, that with sufficient resources devoted to training and propitious circumstances, standards could be raised. Their experience on this project was to teach them that when circumstances were not propitious, standards could equally well be worn down.

In addition to their managers brought in from Hong Kong, HK Building has spent a great deal of time and resources on training a locally recruited team of managers. At the outset of the project, these shared their Hong Kong colleagues' indignation at the standards and mode of operation of the subcontractors and CCG. These were seen as clearly inferior to their 'own', that is, the standards in which they had trained and put into practice within HK Building. Many of these managers had been recruited from CCG itself and similar companies on the mainland. All regarded their new mode of operation as far superior to that from which they had escaped. Nevertheless, by the end of the project many had reverted to their former ways.

This can be illustrated by the case of the safety manager from the HK Building team. Himself a one-time employee of CCG, he was full of praise for the pattern of operation of HK Building that he had become used to on other sites. He praised with admiration the effectiveness of the heavy fines imposed on workers and the insistence of HK Building that subcontractor managers who failed in their responsibility be replaced. He soon found that its CCG partner blocked any such moves by HK Building on the project. At first, this was met with frustration and scorn from the mainland HK Building manager. By the end of the project, however, he had slipped back into a more easygoing stance. This he was then justifying in terms of the need for tolerance of shortcomings and sympathy for the difficulties faced by the workers and contractors. This fitted well with the traditional cultural value attached to *renqing*, to making allowance for human feelings. From the circumstances, however, it seemed that traditional values were here being called back into play as rationalization after the event, putting a brave face on a harsher reality.

The managers from Hong Kong had standards more deeply ingrained and harder to change, yet eventually a degree of accommodation to local norms took place. With the mechanical and engineering manager mentioned earlier, where his protests continued, they were ignored and his influence curtailed. At other times, outnumbered by CCG colleagues, he was bullied and cajoled into agreeing with their decisions on lowering quality standards. As for the general manager of the general contractor, he adjusted the standards he demanded downwards. His argument was that accommodating local standards in some areas would at least allow him to bring some influence to bear in others. In such conditions, improving standards a little was all that was possible and was a worthy achievement in itself. 'How can you expect a rose to bloom in a desert?' he replied in answer to my enquiry about how the project had changed him. 'I have had to become like all the rest in order to have any say.'

Yet his change in heart was not carried out without unease, fearing this would get him into trouble with his superiors back in Hong Kong were they to hear. His anxieties, however, were unexpectedly relieved when, halfway through construction, CCG took control not merely of the project, but bought a controlling share in HK Building itself. With the strategy and ethos of HK Building's operations on the mainland now set by CCG, the managers of HK Building on the site now saw no future for their former way of running the business. Far from the 'international' firm setting the example for the state-owned enterprise, HK Building started to adapt still further to the ways of its new master.

Feeding the poor and less capable child

The owners, at least as far as the German partners were concerned, thus found themselves with a general contractor different from their expectations.

This was to have ramifications not only in terms of supervision, but also in terms of the quality of the construction teams. As mentioned earlier, it was not unknown for CCG to find itself bidding against one of its subsidiaries, as it had in the present case against Number 11. Once it had won the contract, however, it did not undertake the construction work directly, but subcontracted this to another of its subsidiaries, City Number 9 Construction Company. Number 9, however, is widely acknowledged not simply as less competent than Number 11, but as the least competent of all CCG's subsidiaries. Yet, this very incompetence was credited with the award of the work from the hands of CCG. As a retired general manager of another of CCG's subsidiaries explained:

> It is like in a family. Number 11 is a rich and capable child, while Number 9 is poor and less capable. It is natural and fair for CCG, the father to take some food away from the well-fed child to feed the hungry child.

Despite the complexity of the design, the project thus found itself with a subcontractor far from the first order.

Models drawn from family life come readily to the lips of Chinese managers in explaining the relationships within and between related companies in the state sector. This is in contrast to the Germans who never employed family terms in this context. Given the long-standing centrality of family metaphors to Chinese philosophy, this is perhaps not surprising. Nevertheless, it appears more than just an attempt to force a new reality into familiar categories. The relations within and between state firms are controlled by a sense of obligation rather than a sole attention to commercial considerations, obligations that do mirror in some respects those within the traditional family.

Cracks

In any collaborative venture that draws together partners from across national boundaries, differing standards and expectations can sow misunderstanding and discord. One source of conflict that was to plague the project revolved around the attempt by the German owner and the architect to ensure adherence to their quality standards. This is a frequent cause of disagreement in joint ventures in China. Quality standards that may strike some foreign partners as just acceptable may strike the Chinese side as over demanding to an absurd or wasteful degree.

On at least one occasion, however, the boot appeared to be on the other foot. The Chinese general contractor was adamant that the concrete floor to the building should have no cracks. The architect wished the concrete floor to be poured in one continuous slab. This, the general contractor objected, would inevitably result in some cracks to the surface. Far better, they argued, to divide the floor into separate smaller sections and to pour these one at a time. The architect refused, saying that some cracks did not matter. Nevertheless, at meeting after meeting the contractor returned to the point and the laying of the floor was considerably delayed as a result. The foreign side were completely at a loss as to this sudden interest in achieving a perfect finish. The German engineer provided from within German Fair to monitor and advise on the project blamed the problem on poor communication within the profession. Many years ago, he explained, cracks were also viewed in Germany as a sign of inferior quality. However, in recent years it had been generally accepted that they were, on the contrary, beneficial. He tried to reassure the Chinese contractor with this argument, but to no avail.

While, indeed, he had identified one source of the problem, he was addressing his argument to the wrong people. The contractor's interest in preventing cracks sprang not from its own standards, but the ranking scheme employed by the local quality control bureau. A concrete floor poured with cracks was acceptable to the bureau and could even be classed as 'good'. However, for the concrete floor to be graded 'excellent', no cracks were permissible. To achieve less than an excellent grade was considered a severe blow to the career prospects and future success of the contractors in terms of winning further large-scale contracts from the state. If cracks were to be avoided in pouring the floor as one slab, the only solution was to employ large quantities of an expensive chemical. Breaking the floor into separate sections would avoid this. It would also be less demanding in terms of the amount of coordination required. When one member of the Chinese side suggested putting their problems clearly to the Western side, he was told that that would not do. 'They would not understand,' was the response of senior managers. As a result, the owner was left baffled and in the dark, the problem dragging on until one of the local deputy governors got to hear of the impasse and ordered the Chinese side to lay the floor without further delay. The costs of the chemical, he decreed, were to be borne by the Chinese partner.

Another attempt to conceal a clash of interests under the guise of a technical issue occurred over the diameter of the bars to be used to reinforce the concrete. The only size available to the contractor was much thicker than the architect stipulated. Being thicker, they were also more expensive than allowed for in the contract. The additional expense would fall on the contractor unless the architect could be persuaded to authorize a change in specifications. Once again, the Chinese contractor returned to the point repeatedly, arguing that the rods stipulated were too thin for the weight that would be placed upon the floor. The architect tried repeatedly to reassure the contractor that such fears were unjustified, that he was confident that his calculations were correct. Some of the younger Chinese managers at these meetings would say in Chinese: 'Why don't we just tell him that you just can't get that size here?' Once again their suggestion was vetoed by their senior managers, who would tell the interpreter not to translate what had just been said, adding the familiar 'the foreigners would not understand. There's no point reasoning with them.'

Such lack of communication at first gave rise to perplexity then to unease and finally distrust on the part of the German side. Rather than trust being built as each side came to know each other, it was destroyed. Initial readiness to give the other side the benefit of the doubt gave way to straightforward doubt. One important point on this path took place on 15 November, when two visiting technical experts employed as consultants by German Fair met with the engineers of the mechanical and electrical installation company. This was another subsidiary of CCG, City Number 13 Construction Company. The two experts were young and new to China. They were met with a series of requests to change products from those stipulated in the contract. In their place, the contractors recommended others favoured on grounds of cost and commissions. The Germans, however, were simply assured that the products stipulated in the contract were unavailable in China and naively accepted all such assurances without further enquiry. The Chinese subcontractors were happily busy recording all these concessions when Martin Li, the Moreland project manager, arrived on the scene. Seeing what was happening he called the meeting to a halt and took the Germans aside to warn them to be more on their guard in future.

The necessity of such caution was brought home to the German side by one incident that was to become told and retold as a cautionary tale. Braun, the German mechanical and electrical engineer attached to the Moreland project management team, rejected an electrical socket that did not comply with the type specified in the contract. A few weeks later, the installation subcontractor presented another. Braun unscrewed the cover to find inside the rejected brand. Evidently, the contractor had managed to arrange with the supplier to place the inferior version inside covers mimicking the stipulated one. Braun was furious and was quick to spread the word of his discovery among his fellow Germans. The result confirmed a growing impression among the German participants in the project that the Chinese firms involved in its construction were prepared to lie without a qualm. One benefit of all this was, however, that the three German partners were drawn closer together in their Chinese venture, their common sense of being set upon by the Chinese outweighing their domestic rivalry.

This is not to say, however, that there were no conflicts among the German partners in German Fair. Early on in the project, Weserstein sent a technical expert to the project when they heard that difficulties were arising. Weserstein was the most eager of the three partners to have the exhibition hall completed on time because it was the organizer of the prestigious high-tech exhibition planned to be the opening event. However, Altdurf was upset because according to the German Fair founding document, supervising construction fell to its responsibility. The interesting point of comparison here is that the conflict was resolved immediately by reference to the founding agreement. Weserstein immediately withdrew their technical expert who was replaced by one from Altdurf. Weserstein dispatched in his place a marketing manager, an appointment within its agreed sphere of influence. Weserstein tried, nonetheless, to use the manager to keep an eye on things by instructing the marketing manager to report on the daily activities of the German general manager of the exhibition centre. She refused, justifying her refusal on the grounds that this was not part of her job description.

These two incidents stand in marked contrast to the prevailing situation within the Chinese business system. The contractual agreement between the three German partners functioned effectively as a conflict resolution device. Weserstein would have preferred to retain its employee in place, but faced with a complaint backed up by the contract governing the joint venture withdrew him without further argument. At the same time, instructions from the marketing manager's boss to, in effect, spy on the joint venture general manager, were refused by reference to the marketing manager's own contract. Neither case would be likely in China, where contracts do not enjoy a similar authority.

Anchor bolts

Before the concrete floor could be poured the anchor bolts had to be embedded. Each of the main columns of the building would be positioned over and supported by these massive bolts, each over two metres long. In a steel structure building of this complexity it is essential that the bolts are positioned with meticulous accuracy in relation to one another. Should they be out of alignment then the columns would no longer be spaced symmetrically and problems in getting one part of the structure to meet up with another would ramify as building progressed. Great care was thus needed when pouring the concrete floor to ensure that the anchor bolts were not displaced.

Unfortunately, the organization of the construction work was not favourable to such an outcome. Division prevailed. Both the embedding of the anchor bolts and then the laying of the concrete floor were the responsibility of Number 9, but different teams were responsible for both and worked separately and at different times. The teams were composed of migrant workers. Most if not all had no previous experience of building work of any complexity. Protecting the position of the anchor bolts would have to rely on close managerial monitoring. The motivation for this was, however, not pressing. Number 9 would not be in charge of erecting the structure. Any problems arising from displaced anchor bolts would befall others. Not only that, but the principal difficulties would befall Gang Tie. Little love was lost between Gang Tie, the steel fabricator subcontractor and CCG, the general contractor who would have much preferred one of its own 'children' to have done the work rather than having Gang Tie forced upon it by the owner. This hostility was mutual and communicated itself to CCG's subsidiary, Number 9.

As a result, when the first floor was laid, for the entrance hall, several of the anchor bolts were displaced. The Jianli, the Chinese quality supervisory body, raised the alarm and the general contractor attempted to put in place measures to prevent a recurrence. Managers were instructed to keep a closer eye on matters. Unfortunately, the architect's insistence on pouring the floor in one continuous slab meant that pouring needed to go on around the clock. Management attention and attendance tended to flag at night and more anchor bolts strayed out of alignment as a result. Nevertheless, the situation did improve.

The problem remained, however, as to what to do with the deviated bolts. The first temptation was to brush the matter under the carpet and to hope everything would come out right in the end. This is probably a universal temptation. It was not one, however, that the foreign participants expected to prevail. As the American supervisor from the roofing contractor later remarked to me when problems stemming from the altered position of anchor bolts were returning to haunt the project, in America a number of considerations would have probably led to the problem being redressed earlier. First, the contractor responsible for the fault would reflect on the likelihood of one subcontractor after another down the line claiming damages for wasted time and material. This in itself would usually prove enough to persuade the contractor responsible to redress the problem at once. Second, managers from the other contractors who would be affected would have kept themselves informed of problems arising in the early stages that would be likely to affect them later and would have voiced their concern.

On the project, however, it was commonplace for managers from contractors responsible for stages not yet in progress to skip site meetings that they were obliged by contract to attend. The head of the general contractor would threaten to fine those who did not turn up, but never put his threat into practice. To his threats, the truants would protest that the discussions were all on matters that were none of their concern. Those contractors who did attend meetings before their work was underway paid no visible attention to the proceedings, filling the time chatting with neighbours and tapping out text messages on their mobiles.

Shop drawings

One bottleneck that slowed operations throughout the construction of the first phase of the project occurred in the drafting of acceptable shop drawings. In China, as elsewhere, design drawings pass through stages, introducing increasing detail as they progress. In the Chinese pattern, the initial feasibility design is followed by the concept design and then the preliminary design. The final stage is the drafting of the detailed design, what would be known in the West as the work or shop drawings.

In the past, in China, the architect or design institutes employed by the owner drafted all four designs. Contractors would be provided with the final shop drawings and would only need to construct accordingly. This is still often the case, but in recent years the involvement of American architects in a number of projects has introduced variation into the pattern. Principally because of the cost of having American firms take on the numerous detailed shop drawings needed, Chinese contractors have assumed this responsibility. This was the case with the present project. Given its size and history, CCG had its own design institute among its numerous subsidiaries and employed its services to transform the general plans provided by the architect into more detailed shop drawings to guide the construction teams.

The drawings provided by the architect and the associated structural and mechanical and electrical consultants (see Figure 3.2, p. 46) fell somewhere between the Chinese notion of a preliminary design and detailed drawings. The shop drawings with which Chinese construction firms usually operate contain less detail than was expected by the project architect and consultants. There was also a lack of familiarity on the part of the Chinese design institute with designs of such complexity. Both factors combined to make the shop drawing teams feel there was little else that could or should be added to the drawings they had been given. They appeared sufficient for work to proceed. Consequently, they were often returned to the architect and consultants in much the same state as they had left them, with little or no precise specification of what was required.

Confronted with shop drawings that appeared little more than replicas of their own plans, the architect and consultants at first attempted to explain what it was they wanted. However, no improvement resulted. Frustrated, they were later to occasionally reject the shop drawings without further comment, simply returning them as unsuitable. The Chinese shop drawing team after receiving these drawings would simply keep them for some weeks and then return them to the architect and consultants without amendment. Annoyed, the architect would once again reject them without comment, leaving the Chinese shop drawing team angry and at a loss.

The problem was intensified by a clash of cultures concerning quite what the role of the architect should be. From the perspective of the Chinese contractors the Western architect was not acting as a 'proper' architect should, refusing, for example, to adjust his plans to accommodate their problems. Such adjustment would be expected of a Chinese architect, who generally enjoys a much lower status and degree of professional independence than his or her counterpart in the West. The first reaction was thus one of indignation. Realization that the role of the architect in the West was different eventually dawned, but this was itself only one step forward in the learning process, as the contractors were then at a loss as to what to expect of the architect and how to treat him.

Unfair treaties

This, however, was only part of the problem. Even allowing for differences in the professional role of the architect in China and America, the project contract had had additional clauses added to the standard version to give the architect and his associated consultants the power to reject shop drawings as inadequate. Their position was that they were merely willing to say, as they did on numerous occasions, 'I have no objection to these plans' rather than agreeing that the proposals were safe or feasible. The responsibility for this was placed, under the terms of the contract, on the heads of the contractors. This was a constant source of discontent as far as the Chinese contractors were concerned. The American architect and German consultants were, they complained, exercising power without responsibility. Reminders that they had agreed to this in the contract carried no weight. This part of the contract was, in their own words, a *maiguo tiaoyue*, a 'selling the country treaty', also decried as a *bu pindeng tiaoyue*, an 'unfair treaty', forced on them by circumstance. The reference here is to the series of treaties ceding territory, such as Hong Kong and the international settlements, forced upon China by foreign powers in the nineteenth century. Mention of 'unfair treaties' is no mere empty historical allusion, but evokes a lively sense of grievance against past 'bullying' by foreigners and resentment of anything that hints of its return. It can serve to effectively neutralize any feeling of obligation to fulfil agreed terms where foreigners are seen as taking advantage of the weakness of the Chinese to force agreement on them.

The notion that business is business and questions of national identity should play no part in its operation doubtless has much to be said for it. However, it does not come close to describing how relationships were viewed on the project. This is not to say that the Chinese participants presented a united front in their dealings with their foreign associates. On many occasions the architect and consultants found themselves in the middle of a tug of war between the various contractors struggling to get their endorsement of plans that favoured one or the other of the contractors. With the work divided among several subcontractors, the plans were often unclear as to where responsibility for work should fall. At these points the contractors would vie fiercely with one another to obtain an opinion that enabled them to offload responsibility for work onto others. The fighting was on occasion further exacerbated by inconsistency on the part of the architect, one day saying certain work was the responsibility of contractor A, the next, the responsibility of contractor B. This inconsistency may well have reflected lack of deep attention on the part of the architect to being asked to adjudicate on issues that were not his responsibility. His decisions thus failed to resolve disputes, but instead became ammunition to be employed by contractors in their continuing struggles with one another.

Yet, where interests did not clash, deception of the foreigners was considered likely enough to win general approval as to be a source of boasting and merriment, even from among the representatives of the Chinese partner to the joint venture. In addition to approving the shop drawings, the architect and consultants had also to be shown and to approve the samples of the goods and materials to be used. To take one example, the architect wanted the concrete masonry to be Sureblock. The contractor bid for Sureblock and quoted Sureblock's price. However, the contractor presented a sample of another brand, let us call it Notsureblock, for the architect's approval. Thinking it was Sureblock, the architect nodded agreement. As construction went ahead, it was clear that the quality of the masonry was far below expectations. At a meeting with the project management and the design institute, the contractor acknowledged that the material on the site was Notsureblock, but that the sample shown to the architect was 'Notsureblock Superior'. Here on the site they were using instead a lower grade, or, as he called it 'Notsureblock Inferior'. Everybody at the meeting laughed, including the representative of the Chinese section of the project management team. Nobody criticized the contractor, nor ordered that the inferior material should be changed to Sureblock and the work redressed.

This is not to say that foreigners involved on the project were simply regarded with antipathy. Attitudes were inevitably in part coloured by the broader love–hate relationship between China and the West, tinged by the familiar mix of envy and indignation that touches feelings towards nations enjoying greater power and prosperity than one's own. This increased sensitivity towards perceived insults. The commercial department, for example, were in general more cosmopolitan in taste and more favourably disposed towards foreigners than many of their Chinese colleagues on the project. They had, as mentioned earlier, favoured Korean Construction in its competition with the local rival. They were also keenly aware of the shortcomings of Number 9 and it was not unknown for its incompetence to drive them, as it did many others, into pouring exasperated abuse onto its unfortunate managers. In contrast, Croce, the American architect, was generally admired for his professional competence. However, when Croce, perhaps taking his cue from the Chinese, perhaps simply reflecting his irascible nature, also exploded during one meeting with the hapless Number 9's managers, the commercial department was shocked and offended. As one member remarked afterwards: 'Tang Jie, you can speak English, you should stand up and shout at him for us.' At the same time, they were quite happy to acknowledge that Number 9 were useless and deserved to be shouted at. Yet not by Croce. As another concluded: 'I don't like Croce anymore. I think he doesn't like Chinese people and does not respect us.'

The mention of respect is pivotal. Displays of respect for China's achievements or key Chinese values would meet with a gushing response. For example, a German adviser making a polite passing comment on

China's success in gaining the Olympics was surprised to find his remark sparking a delighted round of applause.

Unfortunately, the message was not always put across so clearly and the appreciation felt passed without notice. One lunchtime, for example, the Chinese members of the project team were saying how impressed they were with Braun, the German member of the Moreland project management team. Their admiration had been won by Braun asking whether the moon cakes given as gifts by one of the contractors would last three weeks so that he could take them home to his wife in Germany. This combination of family feeling, a prime Chinese virtue, and appreciation of moon cakes, a venerable Chinese tradition, clearly endeared him to those present. However, just when this round of admiration was ending, Braun entered. All conversation stopped and everyone busied themselves with their lunch. One person whispered 'the foreigner will hate the lunch, the fish is too small and bony for them.' Most people at lunch could speak good English, but nobody initiated any conversation with Braun.

This reflects another factor inhibiting communication. Most Chinese on the project felt ill at ease with foreigners, somewhat at a loss as to how to handle them. Neither fear nor loathing but rather tentativeness born of perplexity seemed the prevailing mood. Part of the difficulty in bridging the gap lay in differing notions of friendship. The Chinese like others employ wining and dining to foster friendship, but friends who accept one's hospitality are considered bound to act in one's favour when in a position to do so.

Initially this was often lost on the American and German participants in the project, who drew a clear distinction between work and leisure. To them, such expectations smacked of a lack of sincerity, of one's company being courted not for the pleasure it gave but the favours it might lead to. On one occasion, the design department was complaining to the general contractor about the refusal by Gutheim, the German structural engineer, to accept alterations to the plans that would have allowed the contractor to claim more from the owner. The alterations were a good idea, the architect admitted, but if adopted should not entail extra cost to the owner. Wu Hai, the deputy general manager of the general contractor, was very upset. 'Why should he worry about the cost. Nothing to do with him. It's because you didn't invite him out for dinner,' he told the design department. I told this later to the head of Gang Tie, intending it as a joke, but he gloomily replied: 'It's no use to feed him. We have fed him many times, but he still doesn't help us.'

Meeting expectations

Another source of friction in dealings with the architect and consultants was the manner in which meetings were conducted. The apparent lack of order, with everybody talking at the same time either to the meeting at large or with one another clearly irritated them, as did the large number of people attending the meetings who served no apparent purpose. In contrast to the architect and consultants, who took notes of what had been agreed, the Chinese participants usually took none. Their memories appeared, however, to be in sore need of them, for they would return to a point apparently settled the previous day and make requests as if the previous discussion had not taken place. To the foreign participants the Chinese managers seemed neither to have any idea how to run a meeting nor the ability to keep matters in mind from one moment to the next. It was clear the architect viewed the Chinese managers as a sorry bunch; the worst simply not up to the job, the best working ineffectively for want of proper management training. On first acquaintance, my notes record I shared in this interpretation.

Rambling and chaotic meetings were not confined to those that included the architect. The meetings held by the general contractor to coordinate construction were of a similar nature. Usually an agenda was lacking or ignored. Discussions would go round and round in circles, with agreement often proving unobtainable. Where agreement was apparently secured, it was frequently not executed. Leading figures would come and go at will or suddenly be involved in mobile phone calls on unrelated matters. A variety of conversations would be in progress all at once.

Yet, not all meetings were like this. In the days preceding one notable meeting with Gutheim, the German structural engineer, the contractors were busy telling each other that, first, questions had to be written down and faxed to Gutheim before his arrival. Second, not too many people should be at the meeting. Third, they should get together beforehand to decide on their questions. Fourth, there should be a spokesman instead of everybody talking at once or engaging in other conversations. All this would have been music to the ears of the architect, who had previously complained bitterly at his time being wasted by meetings that had none of these qualities.

And, indeed, come the day it seemed that the Chinese team had finally learned how to run a meeting. There were no longer the usual mobile phone conversations, shouting at each other across the table, running in and out of the room, leaving the table to admire the view out of the window or simply dozing off. Instead, everybody was attentive and kept reminding each other to keep quiet and to ask important questions only. They also appointed one member to speak on everybody's behalf and another to take minutes. Gutheim was obviously well pleased with this and made a number of important concessions enabling the Chinese construction company to save much time and money.

Nevertheless, it did not last. Once the Chinese team had secured the concessions, the meeting rapidly reverted to a more bazaar-like atmosphere. Over the course of the year, my notes reveal that roughly once a month one meeting out of the dozens that I would attend in the course of the month caught my attention. It would seem as if the meeting was being effectively chaired, sticking to an agenda and disposing of points one at a time. Each time I took it as a sign that the participants were learning to run meetings effectively. However, each time the meeting in question would be closely followed by another that returned to all the old informal ways. Clearly, meetings were informal not because of any ignorance of what a formal meeting should be like.

The formal meeting with Gutheim revealed the key to the matter. The meeting focused on the amount of tolerance to be allowed at key points throughout the structure. The demands of the design were very exacting, even by international standards. It became clear to the contractors that even approaching them would be costly and difficult for all of them. Whatever differences of interest they might have, they were united by the import-ance of the overarching goal of getting the architect to ease the tolerance limits. The coordination of the meeting flowed smoothly from this. In discussing this strategy, some consideration was given to pleasing the architect. The contractors were aware that such a meeting would appeal to him, as, indeed, it did. Yet, the principal criterion was simply bringing all their forces together in the most effective way possible to serve their overarching goal.

It was precisely because there was no such unifying force of sufficient strength that the meetings usually resembled less a meeting to address common problems than a continuing negotiation between independent parties haggling in the marketplace. The problem was one of authority. The German partners in the joint venture had anticipated that this would be provided through the contract. The contract certainly worked in that direction, but, as we shall see, it was routinely overborne, unable to control contending interests and competing sources of authority. This point will be developed more fully later, but staying with the architect for the moment, some part of the problem is immediately evident.

For while on the occasion of the uncharacteristically efficient meeting with Gutheim the interests of the contractors were united, for the most part they were contending with one another for decisions favouring themselves and clamouring for his attention to their needs. The Chinese may prize harmony, but, as far as the project was concerned, when matters of vital interest were at stake they fought fiercely.

Contention arising between the architect and the contractors, backed at times by allies drawn from the Chinese side of the joint venture, were particularly acute over the procurement of mechanical and electrical equip-ment. Personal interest in promoting a particular brand for the sake of kickbacks was widely suspected. With the going rate, freely discussed by Chinese participants on the project, at 3 per cent, vast sums in compar-ison to the small salaries of Chinese managers were at stake. In addition, the contracting firms had a straightforward commercial interest in persuad-ing the architect to change from the international brands called for in the specifications to cheaper local alternatives.

The laissez-faire manner of the meetings we have been considering cannot be viewed as a simple product of Chinese tradition. The Hong Kong managers from the now subordinate HK Building element of the general contractor were frequently to be seen exchanging weary glances and drawing circles on the table with their finger to show their exasperation as the meeting itself went round and round. Comparing practice on the site with that familiar to them from construction in Hong Kong, they would criticize the lack of structure and the length of meetings which addressed themselves to matters that in Hong Kong would be settled between individual managers.

The mainland managers were familiar with a more formal style of meeting, though the procedure was once again of a different order from that familiar to international practice. As part of my fieldwork I managed to secure the opportunity to view a meeting held by Wu Hai back at his head office. He, it may be recalled, was the de facto head of the general contractor, the leading representative of CCG on the site. It was he who had the task of trying to bully and cajole the contractors into collaborating and fulfilling their work on time and to order. Given the disunited team he had to drive along and the lack of sanctions at his command he achieved more than many might. The meeting he chaired back at his head office was in striking contrast to the hubbub familiar from the site. There his subordinates, who took notes as he issued his orders, listened in attentive silence. After the orders were issued, he asked each member of staff whether there were any questions. There were no questions. Earlier that day, back on the site, he had been barely first among equals, a king contending with powerful feudal vassals. Here, in his own office, he was the absolute monarch holding court. It must have been a welcome relief.

The meetings with which the managers on the project were familiar were either kept in order by the presence of a powerful figure or they tended to drift. The notion of authority being vested in the meeting itself and of the chair drawing its authority by delegation from the meeting was an alien concept, as it is in Chinese society more generally. Authority is delegated from on high, not conferred from within. Meetings may be the forums of authoritarian leaders or subject to laissez-faire drift and contention. They may alternate between the two. They do not tend, however, to run democratically. This was evident when a powerful figure passed the chair to someone relatively powerless. Meetings would descend into disorder. There is an unsentimental attitude towards power: individuals with the power to harm receive deference, while those without can expect none.

Enter the governor

On 25 November at 4.30 in the afternoon, the joint venture was told that the special zone governor would come to the site to hold a meeting. The following morning everybody gathered at the site in readiness. At 9.00, the governor's office rang to inform everyone that the meeting was postponed until 10.00 and that the venue would now be at the governor's own office. Everybody rushed across town to reach the office in time. After we had waited for ten minutes in an imposing wood-panelled meeting room, the governor arrived and asked Zhang Haiying, the deputy general manager, to report on the progress of the project.

Her report emphasized all the efforts that had been made to make the situation on the site better, and understated the problems that existed, blaming these largely on the architect. Her speech appeared to please the special zone governor, but Weinmuller, the representative from German Fair sent to advise on the construction, soon corrected the rosy picture. He asked to speak and was granted five minutes by the governor. He said that there were indeed problems of communication with the architect, but that they sprang from the inability of the general contractor to appreciate the intention of the design and Western design language. He also remarked on the German partners' anxiety over the general contractor having failed to finalize contracts with their subcontractors. At this, the special zone governor shouted at HK Building:

> I know all about the story of your bidding. It is like an exciting film, full of climax and surprise. It is not an accident that you got this project. I tell you that if HK Building mess up this project, you will never have another one in this city. I do not wish to listen to your explanation about why the contracts have not been signed. Get them signed straight away.

This outburst left the HK Building head looking anxious and alarmed. His discomfort increased when Weinmuller went on to tell the governor that the general contractor had not handed in its detailed progress schedule. While the complaint was directed against the general contractor in general, it was HK Building who once again bore the brunt of the governor's anger. He shouted at its team, ordering it to attach the schedule to the minutes of the meeting. The local member of the consortium, CCG, escaped any similar tongue-lashing. The governor then went on to tell Steinhausen, the general manager of the joint venture: 'the joint venture managers should also manage well. You should know what is your responsibility, do not always telephone to report to the German side.' This complaint echoed one frequently voiced by Zhang Haiying, that Steinhausen spent too much time and money telephoning German Fair in Germany and did not care to take decisions on his own authority.

The governor then turned to the head of the Chinese design institute acting as consultant to the project and said: 'I know that you will send people to the site every day, right? Your company is very famous, but not every building you were responsible for is in good condition.' It later emerged that the head of the design institute was unhappy with this idea.

The contract stated that the institute had only to provide a representative on the site one day a week. However, he voiced no objection in front of the governor. The governor then proceeded to shout at the Jianli, ending with a homily on how it should do its work well. Rounding off, the governor explained that the deputy mayor under whose aegis the exhibition centre fell as a key municipal project had discussed with him how best the project could be assisted. As a result, the project would be taken over by Mr Chen of the municipal key project office. 'He will manage the project on behalf of the municipal government and organize project meetings on site attended by key project office officials. The governor and deputy mayor will attend if necessary.'

The governor went on to add that the project also had the full support of the special zone and was ranked as the prime key project in the zone. Consequently, the special zone key project office would also take an active role in the running of the project. The special zone government would ensure that all the permits needed from it would be issued by the end of the week. His staff would also assist in gaining permits issued by the next tier up in the government, the municipality. He then closed the meeting.

This meeting was to be the first of many on the project attended by high government officials. Something of the awe they inspired among the Chinese managers of the joint venture and the contractors can be seen in the fury Ma Bo, the head of the project management team, unleashed against his subordinates for not informing him in time about the changed time and venue of the meeting. As a result, he was late. For someone in his position, dependent on pleasing local leaders for his future, this was a grave matter. Managers would counsel one another to avoid coming to the site rather than arriving late when such meetings were in progress. During the meeting, everybody would sit quietly, heads bowed. The tea, the finest quality, would remain untouched by all except the foreigners. Likewise, it was only the Germans and their representatives from Moreland who would volunteer comments without first being commanded to speak by the presiding mandarin. Nobody else would dare to question whatever the special zone governor or deputy mayor said. Such meetings were very much one-sided instruction, ordering and threatening. There is the clear message, stated both implicitly and explicitly, that the leader holds the fortunes of his audience in his hands. However, when the meetings were over and the officials had left, the outward displays of deference soon gave way to the hitherto unvoiced inner misgivings.

For their part, the German participants and their Moreland representatives had mixed feelings about the intervention announced by the special zone governor. On balance, however, they considered it would prove helpful. As Martin Li, the Moreland project manager, remarked to me after the meeting:

> We may be able to make use of the government to push the project along. People are obviously frightened and people here only want to

listen to what the emperor says. What anybody else says does not count. Only the emperor counts.

There was some disquiet that the governor appeared to know nothing about the contract, and issued instructions without any regard to what had been agreed in it, but the full implications of this had yet to become clear.

For everyone on the project, the special zone governor taking matters in hand came as a bolt from the blue. Yet, in retrospect, all should have seen the storm clouds gathering. Shortly before the meeting with the special zone governor, the top executives of the special zone Land Development Corporation, the Chinese partner in the joint venture, had themselves been summoned to a meeting with the governor. The Land Development Corporation had been making losses for some time and the government had decided to seek to rescue the situation. The Land Development Corporation was to be taken over by its sister organization in the special economic zone, the Jinrong Development Corporation, hitherto responsible solely for the financial district. As part of this reorganization, Wang Ke, the chairman of the joint venture, was relieved of his post. This was given to the chairman of Jinrong Land Development Corporation, Du Yinhua.

Opinions varied as to why Wang Ke had been replaced. Some thought the German partners had been responsible, complaining to the mayor about his conduct. The Germans I interviewed all expressed surprise at this idea, which they denied. For them, Wang's dismissal was explained as the quite natural consequence of having headed a company that had failed to make money and had been taken over. Favoured Chinese explanations, however, had nothing to do with poor economic performance, and everything to do with a failure to maintain harmonious relationships with the right people. One popular variant of this was that Wang had spent too long away from his home base within the Land Development Corporation, allowing his rivals to chip away at his position, '*wa qiangjiao* – destroying his walls'.

Whatever the truth of these different explanations, a new broom had been put in place. Immediately everyone returned from the first meeting with the special zone governor, it began to sweep. The Chinese staff of the joint venture and the project management was summoned to a meeting with Du. When the secretary arrived to tell the commercial department to attend, I rose to join them. The secretary stopped me. This was one occasion, it seemed, when my presence was not welcome. My disappointment must have been obvious, for some of my colleagues told me not to worry. They would take notes and let me know what happened. I found myself with a research team.

6 Erection

The commercial department returned from the meeting with Du, the new chairman of the joint venture, looking upset. The style of the new chairman had clearly taken them aback and left them feeling anxious. As one remarked: 'You should have been there to study the real management style of the Chinese. It was like going back to the Cultural Revolution.' Du, it was generally agreed, despite being young and studying part-time for an MBA at a leading Chinese university, was wedded to a leadership style firmly rooted in the communist tradition of ideological exhortation and political campaigns. 'His speech,' someone added, 'was full of class struggle.'

This last comment was intended to convey the tenor of Du's speech. I reproduce a portion here to give something of its flavour:

> The whole company should unite as one force with the attitude that the war has started and we shall fight and win. . . . We should have very strong and strict organization and organizational discipline. . . . We shall have extraordinary work energy and spirit, everybody should know when they have to come to work but should not know when they can go back home. As long as there are people on the site, there should be people here in the project management. No entertainment is allowed at lunchtime . . . I had a look one day at the office, there is no atmosphere that we are facing a war. . . . There should be schedules on the wall of every office marking the target of every person and every office per day, per week and per month. . . . You should have a sense of responsibility. Finish all tasks today. Everybody should know what they have to accomplish every day, and also know what their colleagues have to accomplish. Everybody should know what their colleagues are up to. . . . We shall punish and reward. The general manager should submit a scheme as to how punishment and reward are to be carried out. This is a key project, we can change the generals, but we can also change the soldiers.

To this Gao, the technical representative of the Chinese owner, added: 'How many opportunities can we have to work on such a project in our lifetime? We should struggle to show that we have made a contribution to our society.'

Here there is a blend here of two types of control. One is rooted in the Maoist era, in the idea that instilling ideological fervour can overcome any obstacle. The other is more recent, the threat of dismissal. Managers working in state enterprises have grown used to lifetime employment, with sidelining the worst they have to fear for failure. Demotion is rare, dismissal still more unusual. Yet, it is happening, as the staff were well aware.

The speech had an impact, but not one that would have satisfied Du. Like much sermonizing the world over, its effect was neither deep nor long-lasting. That afternoon the Chinese staff decided to stay late. The extra hours worked were, however, filled largely with chatting and eating. Staying late also held out the promise of overtime pay and the prospect of paid taxi trips home.

Homilies and humility

Along with other plans for the project, the governor announced that two officials from the special zone key project office would visit the site each Wednesday. Two officials from the municipal key project office would join them for a further meeting each Saturday. The governor or his deputy, sometimes accompanied by the deputy mayor, would also attend the Saturday meetings.

In the event, the two municipal key project officers were to act as bureaucratic expediters, taking little active interest in the project except when directed to assist with easing bureaucratic bottlenecks. Their success here was dependent on the strength of the bodies they were dealing with. The utilities, given their monopoly position, are notoriously high-handed. The state-owned gas company, for example, generally refuses to fit in with the construction plans of others; preferring to come along after work has been completed and lay pipe work at a time of their own choosing, regardless of cost and inconvenience. Invited to attend planning meetings with the project construction team, its representatives initially refused to attend. Only when the municipal project management officials prevailed upon them to do so did they deign to attend one meeting held on site by the deputy governor, insisting that their business was dealt with first and leaving early. Throughout their cooperation was courted with great respect. Despite agreeing to attend some further coordination meetings with the contractors, in the event they failed to make any effort to fit in with the work that others were doing. As Ma Bo, the project manager, said in summing up their general approach:

> The gas people normally never come to work on the site while other contractors are digging. The always come after everything is done including the landscaping and then they will open up the ground and lay their pipes. They are bastards.

The municipal project officers, then, had mixed fortunes in their attempts to assist the project. The two special zone key project officers had rather less to contribute, as their status in the government hierarchy left them at too low a level to influence bodies at or parallel with the municipal tier. Their involvement in meetings was largely ritualistic. The Wednesday meetings could not begin until they had arrived, but their contributions were limited. One had little or nothing to say, contenting himself with smoking the cigarettes with which he was endlessly plied by his hosts. The other was something of a high-flyer, unusual in achieving his position in the civil service by direct entry through the professional examination system. In addition to his post as special zone key project officer, he was deputy chairman of the special zone construction committee. His contribution to the meetings was largely limited to making the concluding statement, which consisted of reiterating the points made by the speaker next in status whose rank would have entitled him to making the penultimate summing up. This reiteration would sometimes run through three or more speakers of increasing seniority. Each would feel it necessary to have his say even when he had nothing to say other than to confirm, more or less word for word, what had been said before.

Such repetition would generally be found intensely annoying by any foreigners present, but was taken as only to be expected by Chinese participants. At the level of the meetings themselves, there was a parallel phenomenon, with several weekly meetings largely repeating one another in shape and content, especially in terms of their closing stages. Let us look at three meetings held regularly each week by way of illustration. These were the project management meeting held each Tuesday, the special zone key project meeting held each Wednesday, and the Saturday meeting held under the special zone deputy governor or, on occasion, the governor or the deputy mayor. These three meetings were held in addition to a daily meeting to deal with work currently being executed. The Tuesday, Wednesday and Saturday meetings were intended to provide a medium-term review of progress and planning.

The Tuesday meeting would follow a regular pattern. First, the de facto head of the general contractor, Wu Hai, would report on progress. He would be followed by the Jianli, the Chinese quality controller. The Jianli would frequently raise quality problems that had come to his attention, sparking discussion as to how these might be resolved. Then would come Gang Tie, the principal subcontractor, followed by other subcontractors. Throughout points touched upon might set off questions and arguments. At the end, the meeting would start to be rounded off by Ma Bo, the project manager. He would issue instructions as to what should be done and deliver a homily. This would dwell upon matters such as how the participants should mend their ways, improving cooperation for the sake of the nation and to justify the trust placed in them. He would then be followed by Gao, the technical representative of the owner, who would repeat much the same instructions and add a homily of his own.

The Wednesday meeting would follow the same format, with Ma Bo and Gao concluding with instructions and a speech, to be followed by one of the district key project officers largely repeating their instructions together with a short sermon of his own. The presentation of instructions by Ma Bo and Gao would now, however, be presented in a more tentative tone, deferring in both language and gesture to the presence of the key project officials.

The Saturday meeting would conclude in a similar pattern, only this time the summaries and sermons would make frequent allusion to the presence of the special zone deputy governor. Judging the tenor to be adopted to convey the right aura of humility and allegiance is a fine art. Hitting the wrong note can jar on all concerned. It is an art to strike a balance between showing one is competent while at the same time leaving the last word for one's senior. By leaving something unsaid or phrased tentatively one tees-up the final word for the presiding official.

At one meeting at which a number of high officials were present, Gao, the technical representative of the Chinese joint venture partner, went so far as to forget himself, embarking on a long speech that laid out a number of definite conclusions concerning the problems under discussion. To make matters worse, he appeared to become so lost in reading from his script that he forgot the normal code of behaviour concerning displays of deference and humility. This made the rest of the Chinese participants at the meeting bored and upset. As his colleague commented in an aside: 'He is a very silly person. He said all those things that should be left for the leaders to say. Now what have the leaders left to tell us? He bores us and the leaders won't like him either.'

Any Germans participating in such meetings found the repetition and speechmaking both boring and irritating, offensive to their notions of how a business meeting should be run. The reaction of some was very strong, amounting to a disgust akin to being polluted, forced to put up with some- thing completely out of place. Sprung, one of the more cosmopolitan, was more tolerant, admitting that politicians tended to be the same the world over, but adding that business meetings were seldom penetrated by politi- cians and their tastes in the West. Such speechmaking would be confined to a final opening ceremony.

The way in which political rhetoric and ritual penetrated meetings left the Germans at times wrong-footed in judging when to raise complaints. On one occasion when a deputy mayor was visiting the site on a tour of inspection, for example, the German representative asked to speak and pre- sented the mayor with a number of problems facing the project. The mayor appeared somewhat taken aback by this, given that in the context it would have been much on a level with what in the West would be haggling with a visiting dignitary as he or she was cutting the ribbon or some such ceremonial. The problem was not that lobbying the mayor was not effec- tive. The Germans were to find on a number of occasions that going to the top of the Chinese hierarchy paid dividends. It was simply that they were all at sea with regard to judging the appropriate time and place.

The result was that their Chinese associates regarded the Germans as dangerous loose cannons. There was general alarm that no one ever knew when the Germans might bring something to the attention of the higher authorities that everyone else would prefer to remain hidden. Communication within the project suffered as a result, with contractors, the Chinese owner, and its project manager withholding information about problems from the German partner for fear news of the problems might reach the ears of the civic authorities. The anxiety was provoked principally by the power of patronage in the hands of high officials, both in terms of the fate of individual careers and the award of future contracts. This inevitably led to a concern to present a good image. In addition, there was also anxiety over the arbitrary nature of decisions made on the spot by the local governor or mayor. There was the fear that these would be ill-informed about the nature of the problem and made without any attention whatsoever of the contents of the contract. Once made, however, direct challenge was, for the most part, out of the question. This is not to say that instructions were always complied with, but disobedience took the form of foot-dragging in the hope the matter would be forgotten rather than open objection.

Due to this relationship, there was a general agreement on the Chinese side of the project that reports to the governor and the deputy mayor should be long on the detail of work undertaken and short on problems, other than requests for assistance in speeding official approvals. Such accounts were usually well received, further encouraging this approach. Far from discouraging speeches that focused on general exhortation in place of concrete proposals addressed to specific problems, officials were warm in their praise for ringing phrases. To illustrate this point and the difference in management style it reveals, I should like to focus on one particular instance.

One objective, two attitudes, three relationships and four styles

The instance I have in mind is a progress report delivered by the project manager, Ma Bo, at one of the weekly Saturday meetings attended by the deputy governor. The report was divided into three sections. The first ran through what had been done in some detail and outlined what remained to be done. The second section outlined the problems that remained unresolved in general terms. The third section put forward recommendations for the solution to these problems. The key lay in exhorting all concerned to change their attitude. It was the sort of speech that representatives of the German side found a waste of time, full of empty words. On the Chinese side, however, this part of the report was regarded as exemplary. The deputy governor repeated its main points, checking with the project manager that he had remembered them correctly. I reproduce a translation here:

All parties must have one objective, to complete the International Exhibition Centre project as a whole without any accident and ensuring good quality, handing it over to its owner before 24 September. This is not only the objective of the government; it is also the objective of the joint venture partners. It is not only the objective of the general contractor, but also the objective of all the subcontractors who may only undertake part of the work at different stages of the project. Only when we are clear about this common objective, will we sacrifice, for the time being, our petty interests for the sake of the whole project.

All parties must have two attitudes, both down-to-earth and scientific and earnest. Only when we are armed with these two attitudes, can all the parties involved in the project reach a common understanding over matters quickly and find solutions promptly to any problems that may occur during the construction process.

All parties must establish three types of relationship: respect for each other, help for each other and forgiveness for each other. Only when these relationships have been established, can all the parties involved understand and help each so that each party is able to hasten its pace of work to the maximum. Meanwhile, each party is to make it convenient for other parties to carry out their work so that the schedule of the whole project can be improved.

All parties should establish four work styles: being serious (being serious about making and keeping a promise), being strict (being strict with quality, work procedures and construction rules), obeying orders and being down-to-earth. Only when we have these four styles will we have a more common language and be able to raise efficiency.

We think that the project has reached its final stage. At the final stage, different interests conflict with each other and these conflicts are reaching their climax. This shows that the most difficult period of the project is approaching. If all parties involved fail to work together and to make prompt decisions together, then it is inevitable that we will waste time.

This speech is interesting in a number of ways. It not only won immediate admiration from the political leaders. It penetrated the management of the joint venture, with both the chairman and the deputy general manager eager to have photocopies of the speech. This, they clearly felt, was what a good manager should be up to. However, the continued popularity of this brand of inspirational exhortation is taking place at a time when ideology as a means of motivating workers is widely recognized by the very Party cadres entrusted with the work as the futile mouthing of empty words (Tang and Ward 2003: 68–70). At a time when addressing such exhortations downwards to the workers has become thought of as empty ritual, it still retains its popularity among managers eager to display their talent at honing the well-turned phrase. Now, however, the prime audience for these ritual addresses are connoisseurs among the mandarins. Ma Bo's style of categorizing and presenting key virtues, the three this and four that, is typical of the campaigns of the communist era, but its popularity in official propaganda stretches back into the nationalist period and even to imperial times.

Better not tell the officials

With the introduction of the key project officers into the project and the regular weekly meetings with special zone and municipal officials, the local government assumed an increasingly active role in the project. Henceforth it was to openly treat the Chinese side of the joint venture and the contractors as its agents. As with many principal–agent relations, how-ever, the government's attempts to monitor what was going on remained hampered by those on the ground knowing more about the true state of affairs than they were prepared to pass on to those on whose behalf they were supposed to be acting. To a certain extent there appeared to be an element of willing connivance in this on the part of officials. Reports of progress, of problems well on the way to being resolved, and requests for assistance that lay readily within their power, such as obtaining official clearances, tended to be warmly received. Reports of disputes that lay beyond their power to resolve or of technical difficulties beyond their expertise were less welcome. Worse still from the point of view of those involved, there was a fear that placing such problems before higher officials might result in ill-informed or arbitrary decisions that might compound the difficulties rather than resolving them.

To be fair, not all officials were ready to accept reports that sought to pass lightly over the problems facing the project. On one occasion, the deputy governor invited the deputy head of the municipal construction committee to participate in the regular Saturday meeting. Wu Hai, the deputy head of the general contractor, launched into a report that outlined what had been achieved and outlined in general terms what remained to be done. He concluded by hoping that the government would intervene with the traffic police so that long vehicles belonging to one of the contrac-tors might be allowed to come to the site twice a day instead of once. At this point the deputy head of the construction committee interrupted, asking acidly:

> Does this mean that if the government gets these passes for you then you can get the project built on time? We did not come to this meeting to hear what you have done; we came to hear what the problems

are and we came to solve the problems. From what I have heard, the project is fraught with problems, the joint venture quarrels, the responsibilities of the parties here are unclear, the technical plans are no good and the construction team is not large enough. You need to tell the meeting about all the problems.

Wu Hai was taken aback, as well he might be, for in all the meetings I attended over the course of the year I never encountered another incidence of such a forthright attack by a leading official on the traditional report pattern. Wu Hai had prepared himself for quite a different reception. Speaking at one of the daily project meetings earlier in the week he had remarked on how 'we need discuss with the project management and the owner what can be reported to the governor at Saturday's meeting and what should not be reported to the governor. We have to communicate with each other to reach an agreement.' He also took pains to ask about how many cranes and welding machines there were on the site: 'I do not want to know how many myself, but we need to report these things to the governor to show how much effort we have taken.'

Whenever there was an approaching meeting with high municipal and special zone officials, pre-meeting discussions would take place to minimize or remove the possibility of criticism of those working on the project. The general contractor often spearheaded these preparations. Wu Hai would spend time at daily meetings leading up to a meeting with the special zone or municipal government reminding participants that they should not tell the officials about the problems facing the project in terms of safety and quality. At one such preparatory meeting he remarked:

> We should say that in general things have greatly improved. There have been some problems, but these have been redressed. I know we have many problems on the site and that we should do a lot to stop them. But it is better not to tell the officials otherwise they will spend an hour again like last meeting criticizing us again and again, making everybody bored to death.

Everybody was silenced by this, even Ma Bo, the project manager, who a moment before had been shouting about the safety and quality problems and threatening to report these to the officials.

There was an irony here in that the general contractor was at times hoist on his own petard. On other occasions he could be found complaining bitterly against the subcontractors for hiding things from him. As he fumed at them at one meeting: 'You never volunteer to tell me any problems. You should let everybody know so that everybody can help you to solve them.'

That the general contractor should wish to convey an image of its ability to run the site smoothly is understandable. What is more interesting is the way in which other parties were prepared to connive in this policy. This was the case with the Chinese project management team and the Chinese joint venture partner. It was eventually to be the case with the Jianli, the Chinese supervisory body for quality and safety. It was also the case with officials sent to the site who might be expected to serve as the eyes and ears of the local government, such as the key project officers. The more time that passed, the more the key project officers were drawn into openly conniving with contractors and others to present a good image of progress on the site, fearing that they would be held jointly responsible for allowing matters to slip on their watch.

Part of the reason why information was hidden from the authorities was simply that nobody wished to be the bearer of bad news. One of the managers provided by the Land Development Corporation to the joint venture offered a widely held belief to explain this: 'The mayors,' she said, 'do not look into matters too closely. When they come to think back on a problem they are likely to associate anyone involved as sharing in the guilt, even if they were completely innocent.' This popular wisdom concerning the workings of authority is reinforced by numerous folk tales featuring emperors given to executing those unfortunate enough to be the bearers of bad tidings and folk memories of imperial magistrates who would mete out beatings indiscriminately to anyone unfortunate enough to become embroiled in a court case.

The concern to manipulate the image of the project could extend to the press. Here, once again, the principal object of concern was the municipal leaders rather than the public at large. As a key project, the site was visited a number of times by teams of journalists. On one occasion, a team had just arrived when it started to rain. It just so happened that at that moment a site meeting was taking place. Looking out of the window the Jianli representative noticed that not only had it started to rain, but that workers were still welding. The Jianli was very upset, as on numerous occasions the contractors had been instructed not to weld in the rain on account of quality concerns. So he stood by the window, waving his arms and shouting at everybody: 'Look, they are still welding, tell them to stop.' Wu Hai was also upset, but for a rather different reason. 'Quick,' he shouted, 'tell them to stop. If a photographer takes a picture and they publish it in the newspaper tomorrow, the officials will see and get upset now they know it is bad to weld in the rain.'

This was all prompted by an incident earlier in the year. At Spring Festival, the journalists had come and taken a picture of workers welding in the rain. This appeared on the front page of the biggest local newspaper, with the intention of showing heroic workers prepared to continue working over the holiday, even in the face of inclement weather. The managers had then commented that it was lucky that the leaders did not know that it was inadvisable to weld in the rain. Since then, however, they had become less certain and did not care to risk a repetition of the experience.

Another avenue of information to the higher authorities that needed to be controlled was the minutes of daily site meetings held between the contractors, the project management and the Jianli. As the local authorities moved to tighten their grip on the project, it was ordered that the minutes of these should be submitted to them on a daily basis. It was widely suspected that these were seldom read, but in case they were, an implicit understanding developed within the daily meetings about what should be fed into the minutes. This was that people would agree to do things, even though it was widely recognized that they would not. This usually passed unnoticed, though sometimes the deputy governor with special responsibility for the project would notice that the same issue would crop up repeatedly and ask why it had not been resolved. Other officials were less thorough and the subterfuge succeeded in giving the impression that more progress was being made than was the case.

Not everyone went along with this, however. As with the case mentioned earlier of the official who would not put up with reports full of empty words, one person stood out stubbornly against the consensus, leaving others somewhat bemused as to how to react. In the case of the daily meetings, it was Xiao Bao, a junior manager on the Gang Tie team, who refused to play along. Whereas others were prepared for the sake of appearances to give promises without commitment, Xiao Bao would refuse. When, for example, the meeting wanted him to give a promise that a bed rig belonging to Xiao Bao would be removed within two days so that other trades could start work, Xiao Bao flatly refused to make the commitment, stating bluntly: 'We can't, it is not realistic. Why do you force me to tell a lie? If other people are willing to give you such promises, you can ask them, but not me.'

His stubbornness would usually leave everybody embarrassed. The response was usually to write down in the minutes that the undertaking had been made even though it had not. This was the case with the bed rig. A couple of days later, the question of why the bed rig had not yet been moved returned. Xiao Bao retorted: 'I told you we couldn't. I have never given such a promise, why we are wasting time telling lies?' Everybody looked appropriately sheepish and helpless before such candidness. Xiao Bao would also insist on telling the truth on other topics that others preferred to maintain a discrete silence over. He would state openly, for example, that the delay in the steelwork was due in part to the delay in the civil engineering work. This was widely acknowledged, but seldom openly stated to avoid stirring up conflict. Xiao Bao would say so openly in front of the civil engineering contractor, the anticipated quarrel that others sought to avoid inevitably following. As a result, everybody, including the project manager Ma Bo, was afraid of Xiao Bao's odd and unsettling inclination to speak as he found. Interestingly, Xiao Bao himself regarded his truthfulness as a bad rather than a good trait. Discussing it with me, he told me that it was his misfortune to have been born stubborn and bad tempered.

Of dogs and deference

The need for caution generally felt by the Chinese managers involved in the project when dealing with officials was further highlighted by an incident as construction got under way and the site began to fill with valuable materials and equipment. Gangs of thieves started breaking into the site at night. The special zone deputy governor suggested to the managers that they should have a guard dog. The managers replied that they would organize a security team to patrol at night.

The thefts continued, the security patrols being intimidated by the gangs. The official repeated the necessity of having a dog. The managers replied that they would find a way to resolve the problem and that the deputy governor could put his mind at rest. However, a few weeks later there were more thefts. This time the government official was adamant that a dog was needed and he criticized the managers for inaction and neglect of duty.

One of the managers from the general contractor explained to me the dilemma in which they found themselves. Now that the leader insisted upon a dog, they would have to have one; otherwise, he might bridle at not being given proper respect. However, the notion of having a dog was regarded with grave misgivings. Large dogs are rare in this part of China and, apart from their occasional appearances at the dinner table, tend to inspire fear. They are generally viewed as dangerous and unreliable beasts liable to take a chunk out of anyone unfortunate enough to get within biting distance. Thus, while it was granted that a dog might well frighten thieves, it was viewed as equally likely to savage any innocent worker out roaming the site at night looking for a place to relieve himself.

When asked why he did not point this out to the official himself, the manager explained:

> It is quite natural and easy to realize that a dog might solve one problem only to cause another. Besides, the leader knows that we have many workers on the site at night. He should have thought about the possibility of the dog biting one of them. However, it is precisely because it is such a simple fact that makes it difficult to point out to him. It might make others assume that one is poking fun at the leader and showing disrespect. It is very difficult to deal with officials, you have to think a lot before you open your mouth, otherwise you will offend them and bring down trouble on yourself.

Face

What we have here is clearly a question of face. It should be remarked, however, that while concerns over face are in some respects universal, this very fact sometimes leads to misunderstanding. This can occur whenever notions of how and why face is gained or lost are imported from one culture into another. The operation of face in China can only be fully understood if it is placed in its cultural context, for it is coloured by the particular configuration of institutions and values within which it manifests itself. Foremost among these is the prominence of hierarchy, not simply in terms of values, but also in terms of brutal fact.

In the incident of the dog, it is interesting to note that the deputy governor concerned was widely recognized by those beneath him as the model of a good leader. Unlike his immediate superior, the special zone governor, and unlike the chairman of the joint venture, shouting and glaring did not accompany his instructions. In many ways, the popularity he enjoyed flowed from somewhat the same source as that on which the reputation of the then prime minister, Zhu Rongji, rests. Both are referred to admiringly as *ta shi,* having their feet firmly on the ground, of being competent and not given to putting on airs. Yet, for all that, the managers on the site were hesitant to risk the danger of challenging the deputy governor over the guard dog. He remained, when all was said and done, a leader and as such was automatically entitled to have his face enhanced and protected by those beneath. In his case, inner regard enhanced the demands of showing due respect. Other leaders may be less popular, but the dangers of neglecting outward displays of deference remain all the more acute.

The importance of hierarchy inevitably colours how face is created and sustained. Subordinates automatically 'pad the face' of superiors or at the very least avoid anything that might damage it. Face flows upwards. It is pre-eminently a matter of deference from subordinates towards those in command, a matter of weakness and strength. For those coming from a different system, what are locally inappropriate expectations about face may easily arise. One such incident occurred late in my study of the project, when the first exhibition was at last being staged. With the arrival of the important event, the chairman of the board of the joint venture, Du, started to take over the role of every manager as he sought to direct everything himself. He would call meetings of staff without consulting their imme-diate managers, even down to the level of the cleaning ladies, threatening dismissal for those who did not accomplish the tasks he set. The German general manager, Steinhausen, protested at this. 'Please give me face,' he asked in Chinese. 'I am the general manager, let me manage these things.' The chairman exploded. 'You want face? If you mess up this politically important fair, what face do you have? You want face, you can manage everything, I am going away, and if there is anything wrong, you will find yourself with too much to swallow.'

This incident took place before other staff and news of it soon spread throughout the venture. Steinhausen was universally regarded as foolish in making the request. One member of staff remarked: 'If the chairman of the board wants to do your job, you simply let him do it.' From conver-sations with other Chinese managers, both connected with the exhibition centre and elsewhere, it is clear that it is regarded as usual for bosses to take over the role of subordinate managers. This is seen as natural and not something to complain about. As one of Gang Tie's managers remarked: 'There is really no job description. The job is simply to take orders from your senior and implement them well.'

Given these expectations, there could be no cause for taking affront, no question of loss of face, in the situation that Steinhausen found himself in. There is no clarification of what is under one's own power or what is not. One's authority is not derived from one's position as such. Thus the notion that you can be undermined by your superior taking over your duties does not arise. One is primarily a transmission link. If the boss decides to manage everything, your role is simply to stand aside or to assist him or her. One does not lose face as a result, for this is one's duty.

The general feeling among the Chinese staff on the joint venture was that Steinhausen should have been happy for the chairman to do the job directly as this relieved him of being held accountable for anything that might go wrong. Steinhausen's concern over face seemed to them inexplicable. This was especially so given the widespread experience within Chinese organizations of delegation being subject to instant withdrawal by superiors taking matters into their own hands and bypassing subordinates.

His being an outsider, both as a foreigner and not being a member of the Chinese state sector further complicated Steinhausen's case. For the Chinese, those in command may at times bestow some consideration for the feelings of their subordinates as a mark of benevolence and practical policy. For those within the same organizational hierarchy the twists of fortune mean that one can never be completely certain that one might not at some time in the future need the goodwill of another. Thus Du, the chairman, treated Zhang Haiying, the Chinese deputy general manager, with greater consideration than he did Steinhausen.

On not taking yes for an answer: management by hectoring

The tendency of those below them to brush matters under the carpet and to avoid straightforward disagreement in favour of foot-dragging feeds adaptive behaviour on the part of those above. The more diligent among the officials, such as the deputy governor, would spot matters that continued to receive mention in reports week after week and would enquire into them, teasing out confessions about the full extent of the underlying problem.

On the part of the general contractor in its meetings with the subcontractors, there was also what at first sight seemed an unwillingness to take yes for an answer. Given the habit formed of not making an outright refusal in dealings with authority, agreement to undertake something was frequently not accepted at face value. Particularly if the undertaking was given in a grudging or half-hearted manner, the necessity of carrying out what had been agreed to would be repeated by the general contractor, frequently embellished with threats and curses. This would be repeated several times, each time demanding reaffirmation. Partly this was a matter of judgement on the part of the general contractor as to the sincerity of what was said, of a feel of when 'yes' meant 'yes' rather than simply 'I hear what you are asking for.' The result added to the repetitive nature of the meetings, with it being felt necessary to hammer home a point in the absence of any certainty that it was secure.

The nodes

The intricate filigree roof structure to the exhibition centre was to be held in place by complex steel nodes. With the intervention of the local authority, a number of problems that had hitherto preoccupied the project reached some partial solution. As these problems ceased to preoccupy the attention, others became visible. Such was the case with the nodes. As attention shifted to pushing forward with the erection plans, Gang Tie was forced, reluctantly, to admit at a meeting with the project management that it was unable to provide nodes of the required complexity. Both Gang Tie and its intended supplier, Kangzhou Valve, had clearly entered their bid for the project with little attention paid to their ability to meet the specifications set forth in the tender documents. The technical complexity and cost entailed by the design had earlier led to foreign companies initially interested in the project withdrawing.

Gang Tie had evidently felt no such need for prudence. Its lack of caution can be attributed to a variety of influences. Some reach back into the era of the command economy. There is a lingering Maoist ideological air among officials and within state projects that *ren ding sheng tian* – man can triumph over the heavens, that given dedication and perseverance, nothing is impossible. As with the Great Leap Forward of the past, such ideas when applied to the problem of the nodes were inevitably bound up with international comparison and national pride. The eventual success in overcoming the problem was to be looked back upon with self-congratulation as displaying a Chinese ability to accomplish complex tasks in the absence of the technological resources available to the West.

Another factor was one mentioned in the previous chapter. Familiarity with more malleable Chinese architects fed confidence that if the demands of the design proved too complex, adjustments would be made to accommodate the contractors. If the nodes proved too difficult, the design could doubtless be altered. However, most important of all was the position of Gang Tie as a state company. The search for profit and tightening budget constraints are making their mark, but these are still softened by a belief that the firm is unlikely to be allowed to go under, particularly where losses are incurred working on a government project. Finally, there was the weakness of contractual enforcement, which meant that the possibility of penalties for failing to fulfil undertakings was remote. Added together these factors led to a situation in which it was widely joked on the project that to hit upon a price managers at Gang Tie would 'stroke their tummies, pat their heads, close their eyes – and bid.'

Thus it was that Gang Tie found itself in the distressing situation of having to admit to the meeting, held at the beginning of December, that it had no idea of how and when the nodes could be made. The project found itself facing an indefinite delay. This, however, not only threw the date for completion set by the contract into doubt. Still more worryingly for the Chinese side it likewise meant that the still earlier date for completion set by the special zone governor of 24 September was thrown into jeopardy.

The deadline set by the governor and endorsed by the mayor was to loom ever larger in the minds of the Chinese contractors as the project progressed. Even at this early stage, however, the prospect of failing to meet it spread alarm. Despite the usual policy of keeping serious problems hidden from the authorities it was felt that the grave threat posed by the node problem forced a rethink. To leave telling the special zone governor and the deputy mayor about what now seemed an inevitable delay in the planned completion was viewed as too risky. Better, it was thought, to tell them now when they had not committed themselves to their superiors and made promises to host exhibitions and invited dignitaries to the opening of a building which was not there. The municipal key project officer was brought into the discussions. He, too, advised telling the deputy mayor. He, however, was not prepared to do it. It was a task no one relished, but everyone agreed would have to be done. Summing up the mood in typical Chinese imagery, the deputy head of the general contractor remarked grimly: 'No matter how ugly the daughter-in-law, she must be shown to the mother-in-law.'

In the end, Gang Tie was prevailed upon to break the bad news to the mayor. On the more positive side, it was generally felt that the deputy mayor might well be able to help solve the problem. The Moreland project manager Martin Li was less sanguine. His response was to suggest to Gang Tie that, with their domestic supplier failing them, they should think about buying in from abroad. Gao, the technical adviser of the Land Development Corporation demurred, feeling that China should be able to manufacture the nodes itself. 'Get the governor and the mayor on to the Kangzhou suppliers,' he advised. 'Get the governor and the mayor on to them,' Martin Li repeated, exasperated. 'What is the use of getting the governor and the mayor on to them if they simply can't do it? You can beat them to death, it won't make any difference. This is science, not something a leader can solve.'

When the leaders became involved, they did indeed get on to Kangzhou. The deputy mayor instructed the key municipal project officer to accompany Gang Tie on a visit to the city in which Kangzhou is located to ask the mayor and provincial governor to put pressure on the manufacturer to put more resources into finding ways to cast the nodes.

The other solution proposed by the deputy mayor was to prove less welcome to Gang Tie. As Kangzhou continued to struggle with the problem without success, the deputy mayor ordered Gang Tie to import the nodes. Gang Tie had made some initial soundings on this and discovered that the cost of importing the nodes would be three times higher than if they could be successfully produced locally. So great was the difference that, on receiving its instructions, Gang Tie made the unusual move of openly protesting that this would be too costly. The deputy mayor, however, waved this aside. 'What does this amount of money mean to Gang Tie?' he commented. He clearly felt that the consortium, associated with one of the largest and richest state enterprises in the country, could afford to absorb losses. For officials the notion that 'you are a state enterprise and we are the state,' is still firmly entrenched. This applies with added strength to those that are large and rich, on the basis that 'whipping the fat ox' is the easiest way to get results.

While the gravity of the problem of the nodes had led to the Chinese side of the joint venture and the contractors overcoming their normal reluctance to communicate bad news to the authorities, the German side was initially left in the dark. News would eventually filter through, but it was seldom volunteered. On at least two occasions, I was inadvertently the source of what, to some on the Chinese side, must have been tantamount to a 'leak'. Shortly after Gang Tie's initial confession to its problems with the nodes I bumped into Braun, the German technical adviser attached to the Moreland project management team. I asked him what he thought of Gang Tie's subcontractor having no clue as to how to design the manufacturing process, to produce the mould and to check the accuracy of the cast nodes. Braun grabbed his hair and yelped. Nobody, he said, was telling problems like this to the German side. If they did, they would be very alarmed, as the bank had financed the project and their continuing support depended on the progress of the project. (In the event, his anxiety over the banks proved unnecessary. Talking to one of the accountants, I ascertained that the state commercial banks involved had been ordered by the government to give the loans to the project. They subsequently did not monitor the progress of the project.)

Once the German side became aware of the problem and involved in seeking a solution, communication still lagged behind events. At the beginning of January, I was asked by a visiting German marketing manager on behalf of Dr Weinmuller, the technical adviser to German Fair, about the situation with the nodes. When I told her that Gang Tie was not going to import the nodes, she was very surprised. She said: 'But it was decided at the board meeting. Board meeting decisions cannot be changed that easily.' Events were to prove her wrong. Gang Tie was intent on ignoring similar instructions from the deputy mayor. Those of the board weighed for even less in its considerations.

Gang Tie: internal links and divisions

Gang Tie's own position was complicated by its internal divisions. Due to the poor costing of the project by Gang Tie, considerable tensions and recriminations arose between the partners to the consortium. For while state ownership continues to cushion state firms against the full penalties of poor performance, financial results are becoming increasingly important for the standard of living enjoyed by the staff of state companies. The profitability of projects impinged directly on the size of bonuses. A manager's basic salary is small and sufficient to support only a modest standard of living. Nor is job security completely assured. Managers are well aware that some state firms were being wound up or left to drift into oblivion. The future is far less certain than the past.

Gang Tie is, as mentioned in a previous chapter, a consortium of three partners. The connections between the three are rather complex, with their present relationships shaped by those of the past. The responsibilities of the three partners are shown in Figure 6.1. As indicated there, Gang Tie Group International Trade Company, International Trade for short, was to provide the consortium's commercial department and steel procurement. The second member of the consortium was Gang Tie Group Metallurgical Construction, here referred to in brief as Metallurgical Construction.

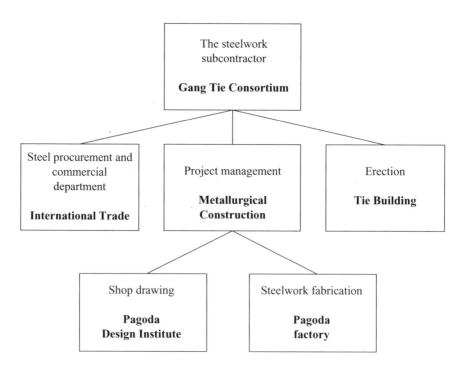

Figure 6.1 The steelwork subcontractor

Metallurgical Construction was to provide project management to the consortium's work as a whole through its own project management department. It was also to provide, through its subsidiary, Pagoda, prefabrication of the steelwork. Pagoda, a joint venture with a Hong Kong company, was also to supply the shop drawing team to fill in the details of the more general drawings provided by the architect. The third member of the consortium, Tie Building, was to take responsibility for the erection of the steel structure on the site.

International Trade is the most financially powerful of the three, being a trading arm of the Gang Tie Group, one of the leading steel producers in the country. Before 1998 Gang Tie had operated as Guojia Steel under the Ministry of Metallurgy. Its foundry in the city was built by one of the construction companies belonging to the ministry, Tie Building. In 1998, however, the state steel industry was restructured. The situation before and after the change is illustrated in Figures 6.2 and 6.3. Guojia was renamed Gang Tie and placed under the Big Business Office of the State Council. Much of

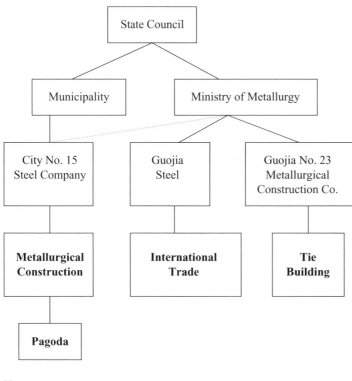

Key:
——— Solid lines represent principal line of control
.... Broken line represents secondary line of control

Figure 6.2 The relationship of the Gang Tie Consortium members before 1998

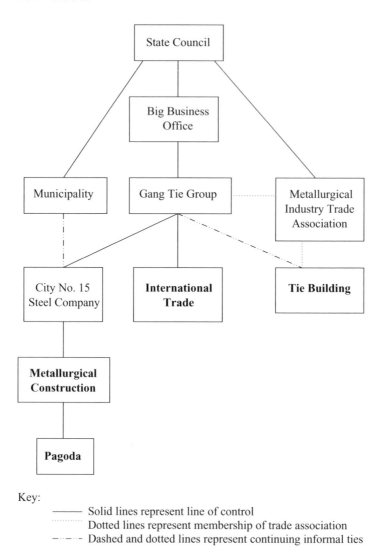

Key:

——— Solid lines represent line of control
············ Dotted lines represent membership of trade association
— · — · · - Dashed and dotted lines represent continuing informal ties

Figure 6.3 The relationship of the Gang Tie Consortium members after 1998

the ministry was transformed into a looser trade association and Tie Building was forced to take greater responsibility for managing its own affairs under the umbrella of the association. Its links to Gang Tie through sharing the same line of ministerial authority were thus severed, though ties remained through personal connections and a certain sense of affinity on top of continuing maintenance contracts. Tie Building also continued under the same Party Office as Gang Tie, meaning that in the event of conflict there was always the possibility of Party involvement to help settle the matter.

Although Pagoda, together with its immediate parent, Metallurgical Construction, has enjoyed economic success, this has not been true of the City Number 15 Steel Company, of which Metallurgical Construction is a part. Overall, the company was making heavy losses. As can be seen from Figure 6.2, Number 15 belonged to the municipality before the reorganization of the steel industry. As part of the restructuring, the city was able to divest itself of this liability, with Gang Tie being persuaded to take the failing local steel company under its wing. This was unremarkable, as successful state companies are often required to take over failing state competitors in the hope that they can turn them round. The local authority continued, however, to retain a sympathetic paternal interest in its affairs and a willingness to assist when this did not clash with other interests.

The relationship between the three partners was thrown into disarray by problems surrounding the nodes. International Trade had been drawn into the consortium on the understanding that Pagoda knew how the work was to be undertaken. It was clearly displeased to find this was not the case. Its displeasure increased as it became clear that Pagoda had seriously underestimated the amount of steel that would be required. Once this was taken into account, losses at the agreed price were inevitable.

These initial miscalculations left little goodwill between the partners to enable them to overcome the inevitable difficulties in coordination they were to encounter. Nor were there any other mechanisms sufficiently robust to make up for this distrust. As mentioned earlier, the consortium itself was not initially bound by a contract and one was only drawn up between them on the insistence of the joint venture. This was limited to one page setting out their relationship in the most general terms. Amendments added at the behest of the joint venture served to throw even this into further confusion, eliminating the possibility that recourse could be made to it as an unambiguous arbiter in the event of a dispute. The cavalier manner in which it was drawn up and amended was a clear indication that the consortium did not look to it to serve such a function.

While all three partners were state enterprises, there was no clear subordination to a common source of control to offer a ready resolution of conflicts. After the 1998 restructuring Tie Building no longer shared with International Trade a common link through subordination to the Ministry of Metallurgy. As subsidiaries of Number 15 Construction Company, Metallurgical Construction and Pagoda did now, it is true, share with International Trade a common master in the form of Gang Tie. Metallurgical Construction and Pagoda were, however, less directly related to the Gang Tie Group than International Trade. Their transfer from the control of the municipality was still recent and the staff had not developed any sense of identity as part of the Gang Tie Group that would serve to bridge any differences that might emerge with International Trade. As the successful wing of the unsuccessful Number 15, Metallurgical and Pagoda were eager to retain as much independence as they could from outside interference.

The strains in the relationship were never far from the surface. One occasion when they broke out openly occurred just before the Chinese New Year, in February 2001. A meeting was convened at the Pagoda factory to inspect three trial assembled trusses. This was attended by representatives of the three members of the Gang Tie Consortium, together with the general contractor, the Jianli, the special zone key project officer, the technical adviser to the Chinese joint venture partner, and both sides of the project management team. The meeting was one of the rambling variety discussed earlier, with no chair, no agenda and participants wandering in and out to view the trusses. It was marked by a lengthy quarrel between Pagoda and Kangzhou Valve, supplier of the nodes. Pagoda complained that it was proving impossible to connect up all the pipework running between the nodes due to inaccuracies in their manufacture. Kangzhou denied this, claiming that the nodes were accurate and that Pagoda's poor welding was to blame.

The steel Jianli, the quality controller, demanded that none of the nodes should be allowed to be used until their geometric properties had been properly measured. This, however, posed difficult technical problems and would be extremely time-consuming. Given that only one platform designed for the purpose was available, insistence on this point would delay the construction schedule by a matter of months, a prospect the Chinese side did not relish given the force of the deadline. This added to the general atmosphere of frustration at the meeting, which culminated in a row between the chief engineer of Pagoda, Ji, and International Trade's leading representative on the consortium, Xu. The chief engineer was evidently very unhappy throughout the proceedings, but did not contribute to the discussion on the pretext of having a cold. At one point in the discussions, the Jianli told the head representative of International Trade that Gang Tie should have done something (exactly what I was unable to catch). Xu replied that he had already told Pagoda about this. At this, Ji exploded. 'You are bullshitting!' he shouted. 'I know you are conspiring against me!'

At this, Xu became rather sheepish, replying: 'Don't be so angry. It is nearly the end of the year. And I am not trying to do anything against you.' Shortly after the meeting broke up, but in the bus on the way back to the site the rift within the consortium was mentioned by the chief engineer of the general contractor, Yu, in conversation with the Jianli. 'There seems to be bad conflicts within the Gang Tie Consortium,' he remarked. 'I think we should not get involved.'

The next day I found that instead of insisting on checking the geometric properties of the nodes, the position of the steel Jianli had changed completely. He was now prepared to allow the nodes to leave the manufacturing plant without his inspection, apparently in contradiction to the Jianli contract. However, nobody from the project management or the joint venture objected, as they were quite aware that insisting on the Jianli establishing that the nodes were in exact agreement with the architect's specifications would mean the nodes would never emerge from the factory on time. That would mean the deadline would not be met. Everyone appeared to hope that the nodes would be accurate or, at least, accurate enough.

Just why the Jianli had relaxed his demands was unclear. Yu attributed it to his warning about being drawn into the internal squabbles of the consortium. There may well be some truth in this. The construction industry in the city is a small close-knit community of its own in which no one wishes to get tarnished with a reputation for stirring up unnecessary trouble.

Assembling the trusses continued to pose problems that Gang Tie was unable to iron out. On the site, the bed rigs Gang Tie had constructed for erecting the trusses lay empty. The general contractor was unhappy at this, fearing visiting officials might comment on the lack of progress. It therefore persuaded Gang Tie that it was better to have something on the bed rigs than nothing. Gang Tie brought in three trusses to place on the bed rigs and held a starting ceremony, the trusses swathed in red ribbons. Speaking to me afterwards, however, they remarked that congratulations were not yet in order, as the trusses needed for the initial stage of erection had not yet been prefabricated successfully. The ones on site should not yet be there and were going to be removed. They were just there to show the officials that work had begun.

In time, indeed, work did begin on raising the trusses and nodes into position. The steel subcontractor was able to persuade the architect to ease slightly the tolerance levels for the nodes on the basis that Kangzhou Valve was incapable of working to the degree of exactitude called for in the original specifications. Having wrung this concession from the architect, however, Gang Tie then became involved in a squabble with Kangzhou Valve over how the extra amount should be divided, Gang Tie pressuring Kangzhou to meet the original specifications so that it could make use of the extra allowance itself in prefabrication and erection.

Just how incapable Kangzhou Valve was when it came to constructing the nodes is a matter of conjecture. Certainly not everyone was able to do so. Kangzhou Valve at one stage subcontracted some of the work out to another company. The results were disappointing, with almost none of the nodes produced by the subcontractor being fit for use. On the other hand, at a relatively late stage, another producer was found, a shipyard in the city. This had no difficulty in producing nodes to the precision required, saying that the nodes were less demanding in this respect than their work with propellers.

There can be little doubt that there were serious problems to begin with, but it was suspected in retrospect by many people concerned with the project that even these may have been exaggerated by Kangzhou Valve to wring better terms from Gang Tie. Kangzhou, as with the shipyard, had experience with the equally complex task of producing propellers. Gang Tie had also neglected to sign a contract with Kangzhou for the nodes, leaving Kangzhou in a position where it could afford to prevaricate. Gang

Tie itself was, however, later content to go along with a version of events that would portray to the authorities an image of Gang Tie managing to solve a problem that no one else had proved capable of tackling.

The rivals

It may be recalled from earlier that the lawyer advising the joint venture on whether it should take responsibility for nominating the steel subcontractor had warned of the subsequent conflict that might arise between the subcontractor and whoever was eventually appointed as general contractor. Assigning control over the steel subcontractor to the general contractor, he suspected, was quite likely to prove easier said than done. This, indeed, turned out to be the case.

CCG, the general contractor, had preferred from the beginning that the steel erection should be awarded to one of its subsidiaries, City Mechanical Construction (CMC). CMC, as we saw earlier, had been one of the firms that had unsuccessfully bid against Gang Tie for the award of the contract. Nonetheless, CCG never tired of attempting to involve CMC in the project and upon being appointed general contractor it employed CMC as its steelwork consultant.

For its part, Gang Tie was also uncomfortable with being placed under CCG in its role as general contractor. From the beginning it complained about how troublesome and time-consuming it was to have to go through the general contractor rather than reporting directly to the project management. In addition, Gang Tie resented what it felt to be a lack of sympathy on the part of CCG, an unwillingness to allow for its position. Gang Tie sorely felt the need for greater willingness in this respect, given its difficult financial situation with regard to the project. As noted earlier, it had severely underestimated its costs and had bid without making proper allowance for unforeseen eventualities. These now began to appear. Gang Tie now found itself pressed by the general contractor to perform tasks such as drilling holes in its steel plate to allow the passage of wires and manufacturing extra pieces of steel for securing the lighting system. Given the additional cost these entailed and the losses it seemed likely to incur on the project, Gang Tie was reluctant to agree, despite its contractual obligation to accommodate itself to such detailed requirements as they emerged in the course of construction.

For its part, CCG was equally ill at ease with Gang Tie. The two companies had not previously worked together. To make matters worse, while they were both state-owned enterprises, they were associated with different levels within the hierarchy. The association of Gang Tie with Gang Tie Group, one of the largest firms in the country and one directly under the control of central government in Beijing gave its managers a sense of superiority over those at CCG and less fear of the local authorities, making them more difficult for CCG to control.

CCG's failure in this area in turn brought it into conflict with the Moreland section of the project management. This came to a head at a site meeting on 29 November, when Martin Li, the Moreland project manager, attacked Wu Hai, the representative of CCG and effective head of the general contractor, for failing to coordinate the subcontractors. Wu shouted back:

> How can we control them? You nominated Gang Tie and forced them on to us. They just shout at all the other contractors, one day this one, another day that one. They told the roof membrane contractor to buy a rope to hang himself, they told the curtain wall people they are going to lose money and told the installation company they are a bunch of useless arses.

At the same time as he was shouting at Martin Li, Wu turned to others at the table, mimicking the characteristic habit of the leading Gang Tie manager of opening and closing his jacket, producing much laughter. Martin Li, on the other hand, was less amused. 'If you cannot control the subcontractors,' he shouted back, banging the table, 'you should not have signed the contract. If you cannot do it, tell me now, and we'll sort this out according to the contract!' 'We cannot do it,' Wu heatedly replied. 'I can write that down, you know,' responded Li, making Wu very upset and prompting the discussion to descend into an exchange of insults. Wu Hai also resented being tagged powerless. 'How could you say that? Without us you would never have been able to start work on the site without all those permits,' he responded, playing on CCG's strength in terms of its local connections.

While the shouting match continued, both antagonists would frequently interrupt their tirade, drop their scowls, and turn to the others present round the table smiling and pointing at their opponent, making remarks such as 'Look at this man, is he being reasonable?' or 'Who is wrong, him or me?' This collectivist appeal to onlookers in an attempt to win them over to deliver judgement in one's favour is a general characteristic of Chinese rows, as much in evidence on the street as in the boardroom, despite weakening a little in recent years. Due to such long familiarity, it is a tactic with which all feel perfectly at ease. In contrast, many Westerners caught up in its use in disputes with the Chinese appear discomforted.

Partly because of these tensions, partly due to pressure from CMC, by the end of December the general contractor was writing to the project management asking that CMC replace Tie Building as steel erector. This continuing pressure to get CMC more deeply involved in the project was well known to Gang Tie. It led to Gang Tie finally speaking out before the district governor in a meeting held at the end of January. Gang Tie were not, its representative made plain, willing to relinquish any of the work, adding that CCG should stop returning to the matter.

Seemingly baulked for the moment in its efforts to win some of the work in progress for CMC, CCG nevertheless had its eyes set on securing the second phase of the project for its subsidiary. Fearing that their detailed plans would be diverted to CMC to assist them in their bid, Gang Tie refused to provide the general contractor with detailed plans as requested, providing only very rough outlines instead. Wu Hai was naturally upset by this, and complained to the client, claiming that Gang Tie's failure to provide detailed plans was due to Gang Tie having no idea as to how to carry out the work.

The general manager of the joint venture was enraged by this and went to complain to a senior manager from Gang Tie. During the course of the ensuing argument the German complained that Gang Tie's slow pace had left the site looking like a tomb, an unfortunate choice of metaphor. For the Chinese side use of such words inevitably conjured up fears of the bad luck such a comment could invoke, making the atmosphere all the more strained. The senior manager from Gang Tie did not shout back at Steinhausen directly, however, unleashing his anger on his unfortunate subordinates instead once Steinhausen had left. Asking them later why they thought they had borne the brunt of the senior manager's anger, even though they had just been protecting the consortium's interests, they seemed philosophical. It was, said one, like children quarrelling. The parents feel they must scold their child for being involved in a fight, even if the child was entirely innocent.

Then, at the beginning of March, the deputy mayor at one of the regular Saturday meetings announced that CMC was to be given the task of constructing one of the halls previously contracted to Gang Tie. This would enable time lost through the difficulties surrounding the development of the nodes to be made up. By the following Monday CMC workers had appeared on the site.

This turn of events came as an unwelcome surprise to the German side of the joint venture. At a meeting between the project management and the joint venture shortly after the mayor's announcement, Sprung, the technical representative of German Fair, was demanding to know who had made the decision, the government or someone from within the joint venture. Martin Li from Moreland said that it did not seem to him to have originated with the government. Who, then? Steinhausen stated that it must have come from Du, the chairman of the board. Sprung was clearly angry. Gutheim, the structural engineer was also present and clearly upset as well:

> I have spent a lot of time and energy over the past half year teaching Gang Tie about the whole thing. It is impossible for CMC to learn about the project in a couple of days and think they can start work. It will also create bad competition and conflict on the site between the two subcontractors.

Martin Li confirmed that signs of this were already beginning to emerge. Gang Tie was busy laying out bed rigs on the sites of the other halls for fear that CMC would grab them as well, 'busy,' as the deputy general manager put it tartly, 'as my cat, pissing everywhere to mark its territory.'

Further problems were developing on the site, with the access roads proving incapable of handling the extra traffic arising from the arrival of the additional contractor. Gang Tie protested vigorously against what it saw as the general contractor's favouring CMC over use of the road, resulting in angry shouting matches at site meetings attended by the two. Eventually, the special zone key project officer present directed the general contractor to get the road widened. 'After all,' he added, 'this is a key project, you should not think about money.' Eventually the general contractor was forced to make an oral agreement to widen the road. It was, however, an agreement given evidently without enthusiasm, and, like so many others of the same type, nothing ever came of it.

Meanwhile, Gutheim and Sprung were demanding of CMC that they submit a contract, a quality warranty and an outline of the proposed construction method. Steinhausen, the general manager, then took the matter a stage further. He issued a letter to the general contractor, circulated to the board of the joint venture. This pointed out that the board had not agreed to CMC coming on to the site to commence work and that CMC was to stop all work on the site until the documents demanded by Gutheim and Sprung had been submitted and approved.

The chairman of the board, Du, was clearly upset by the letter, and at a meeting with the general manager, the deputy general manager and Sprung, made his feelings plain. Steinhausen should not have issued such a letter without consulting him, he complained. It had made both him and the government lose face. Just as to who made the decision to appoint CMC remained, however, unclear, as Du would at one moment state that the decision was the government's and not his own, at another admit that he had started the whole thing off at a meeting with the deputy mayor some days before the mayor's announcement. Steinhausen, he insisted, should withdraw the letter.

Steinhausen refused and the argument continued, Du shouting, his eyes bulging. Sprung also entered the fray, pointing out that when, at the previous meeting of the board, Du had suggested bringing in CMC, the board disagreed, fearing the legal and financial complexities this might entail. Du had then said that he would not really bring in CMC, but merely threaten Gang Tie with the possibility to put more pressure on the subcontractor. This alone the board had agreed to. The deputy general manager, for her part, did not take an active role in the dispute, but was left playing with her watch, mumbling, 'we should not quarrel.'

Sprung eventually took up the role as peacemaker, pointing out that they were all in the same boat and claiming that the letter had much the same intention as Du, the aim was to push the project along by forcing CMC to get everything ready. If that could be achieved rapidly, then the halt on CMC could be laid aside. Du agreed and went next door to where the special zone key project officer was holding a meeting with the contractors. After a whispered conversation between the chairman, the deputy general manager and the key project officer, the key project officer announced that CMC should get everything demanded by Gutheim ready by the end of the week. If Gutheim did not accept what was provided, the matter would be referred to a panel of experts for resolution, as the foreign engineer was not necessarily right in everything. A contract should be signed, but commercial details could be left to later. Everyone should forget their financial concerns and work hard for the government and the project. As for Gang Tie, it was a big company and should behave in a gentlemanly manner and not bear grudges.

Gang Tie, however, was not quite so easily persuaded. It resisted any attempt to reassign work that would lead to it receiving less than it had already contracted for. It held out through numerous meetings until one at which the deputy mayor turned up flanked by the head of the municipal finance bureau and the head of the planning bureau with supervisory power over contractors. Both wield great power over the selection and operation of contractors. Neither contributed to the discussion. Their presence alone was enough and Gang Tie threw in the towel. Later there was to be one last ditch effort by Tie Building to refuse to sign a contract that would cede still more work to CMC. The special zone key project officer persuaded Tie Building to do so, however, pointing out that in words what his colleagues at the municipal level had earlier achieved by their mere presence: 'If you sign the contract now, everything will be all right in the future for you in the special zone. However, if you do not, then things will be difficult in the future.'

For its part, CMC was clearly aware of how much it owed to its patrons in the local government. It paid greater care to cultivating its image in the eyes of the local mandarins. To give the impression of greater speed than its rivals, it craned many of the part-assembled roof trusses into position on the roof without welding them, giving an impressive picture from a distance and the look of outpacing its rival. However, contrary to appearance, speed was sacrificed, as the trusses would have to be removed and rearranged in order for welding to proceed. Similarly, when it came to campaigns orchestrated by the local government, CMC put out many banners and slogans in contrast to the one token banner contributed by Gang Tie, which evidently felt less need to flatter the local officials by such displays.

Problems of coordination continued. Gang Tie found itself having to dismantle bed rigs originally designed to be wheeled efficiently upon completion of one hall to the next as it found itself hemmed in by CMC's scaffolding. This proved costly and time-consuming.

As the managers from both sides became more used to dealing with one another, attempts were made to coordinate with the realization that, regrettable though the presence of their rival was, each side would benefit from some cooperation. Such attempts, however, were at times foiled by hostility remaining between the workers from the two sides, who would refuse to release materials to the other side or to make way for their rival as arranged for by their managers. Feelings of rivalry between the two workforces had been present from the arrival of CMC on the site, and the workforce had not had the experience of daily meetings with the other side to produce the same degree of understanding, however grudging, to be found among the managers.

Even among the managers, however, there was no smooth development of cooperation. My notes reveal a pattern where one week's apparent progress in learning how to cooperate was followed by another in which meetings reverted to managers shouting themselves hoarse and becoming increasingly frustrated as agreement eluded them. Part of the problem lay further back in the production process, with the uncoordinated production of the steel parts. In order to meet the tight schedule, Pagoda was forced to subcontract some of the prefabrication work. This went to firms without any computer management systems, leading to Pagoda losing touch with what was being delivered direct to the site by these subcontractors. Parts which were not needed until later were turning up, while there was a shortage of material needed at once, leading to problems as to who should get what.

Not amused

Despite these difficulties, work moved forward, and CMC was awarded additional work in order to try to meet the deadline for completion of the steel erection. In addition to its first hall, it was given another. Finally, it met together with Gang Tie on the final hall left to be erected, each side taking half the hall each. The contrast between the two sides was plain for all to see, with CMC relying on completely scaffolding its half of the hall and Gang Tie relying on bed rigs. How they would succeed in getting both sides to join up was a source of wry comment for the German side of the venture. Some of these filtered back to Germany, where someone produced the cartoon shown in Figure 6.4, pencilling in the names of key players on the project, such as Sprung, Martin Li and Ma Bo above the heads of the supervisors scratching their heads over the misaligned rails.

This was faxed to Sprung, who showed it to the contractors, expecting them to find it funny. Unfortunately, Sprung had failed to allow for humour being a poor traveller. While nothing was said to his face, a very dim view of the cartoon was taken by the contractors, who saw it as a deliberate insult on the part of the Germans rather than for the harmless good fun that was clearly intended. For while such a cartoon might well appear in some Western countries as a piece of enjoyable self-mockery, it would not have made an appearance from among the Chinese staff on the site, except

Figure 6.4 The cartoon

possibly as a deliberate insult to an opponent. Once Sprung had left, the Chinese managers to whom he had shown the cartoon were livid. They seldom missed an opportunity subsequently to mention with bitterness the perceived insult. When CMC and Gang Tie finally finished, Wu Hai from the general contractor announced with evident satisfaction (and possibly relief) that 'unlike what the Germans claimed with their cartoon, we have successfully linked the two sides.'

Before this could happen, however, another thorn was introduced into the flesh of the contractors with the arrival of a new member of the Moreland project management, George Wells.

7   Completion

George Wells, an American, was added to the Moreland contingent on the project management team in response to anxiety of the German client that quality was being sacrificed in the rush to meet the deadline set by the local government. He arrived full of enthusiasm, assuring the contractors that, as he put it, 'I am not here to criticize you, but to give you support.' At first, all seemed well, with mutual assurances of goodwill and Wells liberally dispensing the large cigars he habitually smoked. When the effective head of the general contractor, Wu Hai, assured him that 'as soon as I saw you, I felt as if we were brothers' it seemed that a new era of peace and harmony between the two sides might be in prospect. It was not to last.

Shortly after his arrival, some of Wells' superiors from Moreland visited the site. What they saw was a deep embarrassment to Wells, with workers seen climbing up the side of a crane in the rain without any protection and dumping debris over the edge of work platforms without attention to what lay beneath.

That Wells should have felt responsibility for these matters, which were largely a matter of safety rather than his particular remit, quality, is at first sight somewhat odd, for Moreland had a Chinese manager charged specifically with looking after safety already on the site. It is, however, symptomatic of a tendency within Moreland in China for foreign managers to assume a position of authority over Chinese colleagues operating along-side them at the same level within the organizational hierarchy. This appeared to receive tacit backing from the firm itself. Partly this appeared to spring from a perception that locally employed staff might be more easily prevailed upon by contractors to go easy on them in disputes with foreign clients. There was occasionally an element of truth in this. Some Chinese staff evidently felt a divided loyalty, as in the case of one junior member of the Moreland staff on the site, who responding to the site memos threatening to impose penalties for poor work that Wells was later driven to issue, remarked: 'only a foreign manager could do it. I cannot. Being Chinese, I have to be on the side of the Chinese.'

Not all Chinese staff from Moreland were so pliant, however, and it appeared that there was another reason why foreign managers felt they had the right or duty to instruct Chinese managers at the same level as themselves. This lay in the assumption that they were there to bring the locally employed staff into line with Western practice. This feeling of being the foreign expert with a general rather than a specific responsibility was doubtless reinforced by the higher salary levels given to foreign managers in comparison with local staff operating at the same level. All these factors combined to produce a degree of resentment among local staff at the powers assumed by their foreign colleagues.

Rightly or wrongly, then, Wells felt that he had been let down. He had told his new found 'brothers' among the contractors about the visit of his superiors to the site and it seemed to him that no effort had been made to make a good impression. It was with a long face that he met them at the next meeting. The brief honeymoon was over. He clearly felt that matters needed to be tightened up. His attempt to do so was to bring him into conflict with a range of participants in the project.

His resolution made itself felt first at the daily site meetings. Wells introduced an unnerving habit of insisting on talking about problems that everyone knew about, but nobody cared to mention. The response was to try to stop him or to move the discussion on to something else. Wells, however, was tenacious. Unlike anyone else, he took what was stated at meetings at face value. In the absence of adequate minutes he provided his own, noting what was said and enquiring at the next meeting whether what had been agreed upon had been carried out. This had some impact. Contractors began to pay more attention to the undertakings made at previous sessions of the daily site meeting. On the things they could do, the contractors did as they had promised. Nevertheless, when it came to more difficult issues, they would still say that they would do them tomorrow, while seldom doing so. The result was that the Wells' list grew and grew, until it contained over forty items. He still clung tenaciously to ploughing through these, to the general irritation of the other participants. One result was an agreement that new problems arising would not be discussed in front of Wells, for fear they would find their way on to the list and result in what had come to be looked upon as his incessant nagging. Consequently, meetings where he was present shortened, only to be reconvened later in his absence.

Wells' outspokenness was not only unwelcome among the contractors. It also brought him into conflict with the Chinese side of the project management team. At one project management meeting at the end of May when I was assisting with translation, Ma Bo, the project manager, instructed me not to translate to Wells what he was about to say. He then proceeded to complain that

> Wells has written a letter to the joint venture saying that the September deadline has made the quality and safety situation on the site deteriorate. I said that he could send the letter in his own name, but he could not send it in the name of the project management. His views distort

the facts. The fact is that the steel structure has been erected, a great battle has been won, and a great achievement made. This nobody can deny. There are some problems with quality, but these are minor compared to our achievement. However, these people do not understand the nature of key projects, they describe everything in a negative way and paint everything black.

These remarks having successfully fanned the flames of anti-foreign sentiment, everybody started to complain about the foreign participants in the project. Gang Tie representatives said that they had never met such unreasonable architects. Wu Hai complained once again about the cartoon. Wells asked me what they were talking about and I told him that I had been asked not to translate. He left immediately, later writing a letter to the German partner, German Fair, complaining. This placed me in a rather delicate situation for a while, as my honesty pleased nobody, with Ma Bo feeling that I should, as a Chinese interpreter usually would, have glossed over what was being said.

George Wells' approach also brought him into conflict with the commercial department. This department, it may be recalled, was working under the direction of the project management. Given the divided nature of the project management, it found itself having to please both Ma Bo and Martin Li, whose positions were often at odds. Wells introduced another element of tension by instructing the department to cut progress payments to contractors who had failed to carry out the instructions of the architect and failed to redress faulty work. Apart from the additional work this would entail for the commercial department, its members found themselves placed under increasing cross pressures. As the first port of call for contractors seeking payment, the commercial department would have to fend off their pleas. This was made more difficult as the Jianli had already verified the amount to be paid for the work, even though it should not have done so before the necessary rectification work had been completed. Wells had also mentioned to the department that he was not confident that project manager Ma Bo would agree to his demand. To this was added their conviction that the contractors would never be able to achieve the quality standards Wells insisted on. The result was a consensus that Wells was '*fengle* – crazy'. When they asked me why he behaved in such an unreasonable way, I suggested that if he did not behave in such a fashion back home in America, he would risk dismissal, to which all shouted: 'But this is China!' For his part, Wells was surprised to come up against resistance from the commercial department on the grounds that what he had in mind was unfair.

Despite initial setbacks, the contractors periodically resumed their attempts to establish ties of friendship with Wells that would obligate him, in their eyes, to place the norms of the group before the rules of the contract and to display tolerance and forbearance in his dealings with them. These attempts were encouraged by Wells' response. Naturally sociable, he was more than willing to develop friendships with his Chinese associates, drinking and dining with them after work. However, his notion of friendship was clearly rooted in a different world and the result was disappointment for all concerned. The other senior Moreland manager, Martin Li, originally Chinese but now Canadian, was more circumspect, maintaining his distance to avoid the indebtedness attendant on such friendship.

In other ways, however, Martin Li was closer to the Chinese contractors in terms of being more willing to bend to accommodate their position, attempting to temper contractual obligation with a sense of fairness. Comparisons in such terms are inevitably a matter of degree. I had been impressed throughout my work on the project by the businesslike approach of Li in comparison with Ma Bo, the project manager appointed by the Chinese side of the joint venture. Martin Li was invariably more concerned with pressing for adherence to the contract. He was known as someone who would speak his mind and was admired for his hard work and integrity. It therefore came as a surprise to me in conversation with Moreland managers from elsewhere to hear some thought him too passive in his approach. They may have had in mind the more confrontational approach of someone like Wells as their point of comparison, though whether this was to prove more effective is, as we shall see, a moot point.

Shortly after his arrival, Wells was present at a meeting convened to discuss a problem holding up the glass installation work. The problem concerned the erection of the mullions to run alongside the glass curtain walls. Like many other aspects of the building, these had been designed by the architect with the view of creating elegance through pushing materials to their limits. As a result, the mullions, while made of steel, were light and prone to distortion without careful handling. Unfortunately careful handling on a site dominated by unskilled labour and inadequate supervision was not to be their lot, and many of the mullions were badly bent as a result. Glazier, responsible for hanging the glass wall, was pressing Gang Tie to redress the problem to allow it to proceed. Otherwise, there would be problems when it came to fitting the glass.

The meeting started with the chief engineer of the general contractor addressing the meeting:

> At our last meeting, we decided that the deviation allowable for the mullions should be 10mm. However, Gang Tie wrote to say that they disagree and Glazier is complaining that Gang Tie is making no effort at all to redress the problem. So we need to sit down with the Jianli, Glazier, Gang Tie, the general contractor and the project management to decide what degree of deviation we can accept for the glass wall and then what deviation is acceptable for the mullions.

At this point Wells intervened. Such a proposal was quite out of order, he insisted, arguing that:

There should be no discussion on this matter. There is only one standard and that is either the architect's or the code. The project management, the Jianli and the general contractor should not participate in any discussions that would have the effect of undermining these standards. Any deviation exceeding those already established should be redressed. If they are not, the Jianli should not approve the work and the owner will not pay for the work.

The meeting continued nonetheless, the Chinese greatly annoyed at this attempted intervention in their normal mode of dispute resolution and muttering to one another about how bad Wells was.

Undaunted by this experience, Wells continued to insist on pursuing deviations from the contract and doing so in a formalistic manner. This entailed issuing frequent site memos to the contractors. The memos were framed in an impersonal and bureaucratic manner. They would state the precise terms of the contract the contractor had failed to meet and cite the contract on the right of the engineer, the project manager, to direct the contractor to redress the defects and the penalties attached to not doing so. Most failed, nonetheless, to have immediate effect, as often the contractors were at a loss as to how to redress the problems alluded to, such as correcting the deviated anchor bolts.

Once again, a comparison with the approach of the other Moreland project manager, Martin Li, is instructive. Instead of issuing site memos on the matter of the mullions, he raised the matter at a Saturday meeting, starting by saying he is afraid the board was losing its confidence in the contractor. This loss of confidence was rooted in the problem of the mullions. He therefore suggested that the contractors should redress the mullions before the next board meeting so that the board could begin to rebuild its confidence in them, something particularly important as the board would be considering whether and how to proceed with Hall 5.

Despite the difference in their approach, when questioned Martin Li said that he thought Wells had at least brought some improvements. Even if only one of the ten things for which he asked was done, that was better than nothing. Asking Sprung, the technical representative of German Fair, what he thought of Wells' blitz of site memos and accompanying threats of penalties for non-compliance, he said he thought nothing would come of them in the end. In this he was partly right, though they did collectively serve as a lever, the claims for compensation under the contract eventually being waived in exchange for an agreement under which the subcontractors agreed to carry out rectification work over which disputes had raged.

George Wells left the project after six months to move to another Moreland project. His replacement, a Malaysian Chinese, was greatly preferred by the contractors and the Chinese side of the project management team. When asked why, the following anecdote was offered by way of illustration. During the bidding for the landscaping, Ma Bo told the new technical manager from Moreland that he thought they should only consider three out of the five firms tendering. At first he said this was because the three were the cheapest, upon which the technical manager pointed out that the cheapest were not necessarily the best and that it was important to consider all bids carefully to determine who could deliver the best work with a reasonable price. Ma Bo then added that the three firms had each been recommended by an important official. Upon hearing this, the new technical manager stopped questioning the move and left the office. The head of the commercial department, recounting the anecdote, concluded: 'Now, if that had been George Wells, there would have been a big row and he would have reported to the Germans!'

This incident happened after my period of observation had ended, so I cannot in all fairness to the new manager attest to the accuracy of this tale. Nevertheless, regardless of its accuracy, its retelling was well received among the Chinese staff and illustrates what is regarded as 'good' management in their eyes in the circumstances of the joint venture. This even penetrated the junior Chinese staff on the Moreland team, with one commending the new technical manager as 'much better, very quiet working on his own, not sticking his nose into other people's business, not bossing people around, not arguing.'

Similarly, though no one involved in the project knew the real reason for the departure of Wells, the explanations put forward are revealing. According to Zhao Wenyan, the interpreter and personal assistant to Ma Bo, it was because Wells could not agree with Ma Bo. Naturally, it was bad to have such conflict within the project management all the time, so Wells had to go. Zhao Wenyan did not pretend to know how this was achieved, but guessed Ma Bo together with the Chinese side of the joint venture had put pressure on the Germans and Moreland to have him removed.

According to Sprung, however, the German side had received no pressure for Wells to be removed. He did not know why Wells had left, but guessed it was out of frustration at no one listening to him. This difference in attributing responsibility for managerial changes is similar to the situation with the removal of the first Chinese chairman of the board. When asked to speculate why this had come about, Chinese managers on the project attributed his fall to enemies undermining his position, the Germans to his lack of success in running a profitable firm. On the one side there appears a tendency to reach first for an explanation in terms of failed relationships, on the other to think of difficulties related to task performance.

Finally, it is interesting to note what George Wells felt he had learned from the experience, his first as a project manager in China. He started by saying that he knew that project management was 5 per cent related to technical issues and 95 per cent related to people. That was the same the world over. However, what he had learned from the project about work in China was that one had not only to deal with subordinates, but also to be adept at handling superiors and government officials. He now saw that one needed to keep the officials at arm's length, not telling them everything nor showing them everything and keeping them away from certain people. One had to be careful not to let them micro-manage every-thing. He had come a long way indeed from the newcomer who six months before had been asking why things were being withheld from the local officials.

Put out more flags: management by campaign

While Wells was busy looking to the contract as the means of ensuring that quality concerns were not forgotten in the rush to meet the deadline, the Chinese participants in the project were being drawn along a more familiar path to resolve their disputes and to unite their efforts. This was to be achieved by the launch of a campaign.

Some characteristic features of campaigns had long been apparent on the project. There had from the beginning been a disposition among the Chinese managers to describe progress in terms of military metaphors, of wars to be waged and battles to be won. Such metaphors were noticeably absent from the lips of the foreign partners or their project managers. Another feature was the flags and banners that bedecked the outside of the building with glowing promises from this or that contractor to meet the deadline while producing work of the highest order and ensuring safety standards. These were ever present, but would increase in number whenever an important official was due to visit. Once the campaign proper began on site, the site campaign committee would confer with an office of the municipality devoted entirely to such matters, the campaign office, to enquire about the latest recommended slogans. Contractors would be advised on these before sub-mitting their proposed slogans to the site campaign committee for approval, a practice that accounted for a certain similarity in slogans to be seen adorn-ing sites throughout the city as fashions changed under the direction of the campaign office.

All municipal and district key projects are expected to run a campaign at some point, presumably in the hope that this will produce results commen-surate with their importance to the city. Around the middle of April, it was decided that it was about time that the site should launch its own. At this point, the special zone key project officers came into their own. Hitherto, they had not really offered much independent advice of any value to solv-ing the problems faced by the project. However, when talking about the proposed campaign it was evident that they suddenly were much more at ease and in command of their subject, describing enthusiastically and at length how to conduct the campaign. They might not know much about technical matters, but here they were once again back on familiar ground.

A campaign leadership team under Du, the chairman of the joint venture, was set up. This team presided over a campaign office headed by Gao, who had been sent to the joint venture by the parent company of the

Chinese partner. Originally, it was believed that he enjoyed considerable power and he was accorded considerable deference as a result. As doubts began to spread about the extent of his influence and it became clear that he had not much practical advice to assist in solving the problems faced by the project, this deference began to wane and he found his presence and opinion no longer courted. He therefore welcomed the chance that the new post afforded to raise his profile and threw himself into directing the work of the office with gusto. Its other members were Ma Bo, the project manager, Wu Hai, the head of the general contractor on the project, Shen, from Gang Tie's project management, and Li Jie, an assistant to the deputy general manager of the joint venture. Most of the work of producing the plans for the campaign fell to Li Jie.

Fortunately, for Li Jie, she was not left solely to her own devices. As mentioned above, the local authority has a campaign office and this provides advice on how to run campaigns and models for guidance. These serve as templates upon which each individual project can draw, adding small improvisations of their own, mentioning peculiar circumstances here and adding an additional target there. Long exposure to such campaigns leaves the task of reproducing the impressive amounts of documentation that surround them less daunting than might appear at first sight. Nevertheless, those who are skilled at innovating while remaining true to the traditional form win admiration and emulation, as we saw earlier from the reception accorded Ma Bo's speech before the local leaders.

In general, however, copying is the norm, cutting down on the amount of time and thought needed. This would otherwise be immense, as the organization of the campaign at the level of the project was, as is usually the case, to be duplicated down into the constituent elements, with each contractor required to establish a campaign leadership committee and office and to feed back to the project campaign office documents outlining its campaign proposals and progress. In the event, most of the structure thus created was more nominal than real, most of the work descending onto the shoulders of the unit counterpart to Li Jie. They would serve to reflect back the rhetoric they were busy copying, most notably in the drafting of the speeches that section heads would present at the meetings called to mark the progress of the campaign.

The document outlining the scope of the campaign and the methods it was to employ was drawn up in the middle of April. This identified the target of the campaign as completing the work on time while ensuring safety and quality. The campaign was to contribute to this by cultivating 'four grasps, four competitions and four spirits'. All were urged to grasp ways of advancing management; civilization; science and technology; and clean government. With this in mind, they were to compete in four ways that would contribute to the success of the project, competing in terms of quality; speed; safety; and cooperation. To do so, they needed the right spirit. This entailed enhancing their sense of unity; their fighting spirit;

their spirit of devotion; and remaining down-to-earth. Almost all the points mentioned echo catchphrases promoted by national leaders, such as the emphasis placed on spiritual civilization by President Jiang.

The plans drawn up, the structure in place, the campaign was inaugurated at a meeting on the site presided over by the deputy governor. All the managers attended, the contractors seated in front of a contingent of their workers. There was a certain theatricality to the whole affair, with the workers quite unnecessarily keeping their safety helmets on in the hall throughout the meeting, The managers each took it in turns to deliver a prepared speech declaring their dedication to meeting the aims of the campaign. These ringing declarations were usually accompanied by dramatic attention to delivery, with tone of voice and gesture pressed into conveying emotional commitment and sincerity. Once off stage, however, the managers would later laugh at themselves, clearly regarding their part as the performance of a role rather more sound than substance.

The workers in the audience seemed equally unimpressed, many nodding off in the middle of speeches to display an uncanny ability, doubtless born of long experience of similar events, to wake up and clap when a speech came to an end. The managers, however, seemed quite unperturbed by this section of the congregation dozing during the middle of the sermon. What was important was to be able to perform the ritual, and the eye they wished to catch was that of aficionados in such matters, the local mandarins. For this reason, despite their willingness to mock such meetings, almost all managers were anxious to ensure that they could participate. Managers would vie with one another to make speeches. Despite part of their ostensible purpose being to motivate the workers, campaigns nowadays appear largely run not only by managers and officials, but also for managers and officials. The workers may put in a token appearance, but they appeared largely indifferent to the ritual being performed. This can be set against a broader national trend for Party members to be increasingly drawn from the ranks of management.

The campaign appeals to self-sacrifice in favour of the common good were not to be conducted entirely in the absence of incentives. These were both material and honorific. Exemplary individuals and units were to be selected and awarded with various titles such as 'windows of civilization' and 'construction heroes'. There was even an award allocated for 'good home helper', intended for the manager's wife who offered most support to her husband working long hours on the project by relieving him of domestic duties.

The performance of the various units was to be monitored by the weekly award of flags on a campaign office chart, with red for excellent, yellow for good and green for normal. For the first month, the chart had many red, some yellow, and one or two green flags. This did not mean that everything was going well. Construction continued to be plagued by quality and safety problems, and there was no sign that the deadline could be comfortably met.

It was against this background that the special zone key project officer, inspecting the chart, noticed that almost every team was being given either a red or a yellow flag. He shouted at the managers present, complaining that the wall chart was not reflecting the real situation on the site. He wanted to see the teams performing badly penalized. It was agreed that black flags would be introduced for the purpose. The next week, a black flag duly appeared on the chart. It was to remain, however, left to one side and never put to use.

Despite this display of monitoring, at the end of the campaign titles and awards were distributed with no noticeable attention to performance. Gang Tie, for example, was allocated three awards, simply on the basis that it had three constituent elements, and was asked to recommend a recipient from each. Here as elsewhere the policy of taking it in turns to receive the awards meant that whether one received one depended on one's position in the queue and seniority, with little or nothing to do with performance on the project. As a result one had senior managers who rarely visited the site and who had contributed little to the work receiving awards for their contribution, while lower-level managers well known for the hard work they had put in were passed over unrecognized.

A similar lack of attention to performance marked the distribution of a batch of municipal and special zone awards for good management. Towards the end of the first phase of the project, the special zone key project officer arrived on the site to announce that he had been given a quota of awards to be distributed within the project. This was promptly decided by a group of senior Chinese managers, including Du, the chairman, Zhang Haiying, the deputy general manager, Ma Bo, the project manager, and the special zone key project officer. As with anything to do with such matters, the German side and their project manager were not consulted. From this dividing up of the spoils, Ma Bo emerged extremely pleased with himself, it having been decided that the project management would take the title of 'excellent municipal unit' for itself. As he went round each division of the project management spreading the good news he also instructed each to write a short essay stating why it deserved the honour. Writing such assessments is characteristic of all such awards, giving the impression, frequently justified, of the assessment following rather than preceding the award. This was also to be the case with the award of the title as exemplary wife. Monitoring being completely beyond the capacity of those allocating the award, the winner is expected to provide the justification for it after the event in an essay of self-praise.

As with the declining involvement of workers in the Party and as active participants in the campaigns, the pattern of awards has taken a similar path. On the site, the accolades went not to heroes of labour, but to heroes of management. This seems characteristic of a shift in China more generally, the era of the model worker giving way to that of the self-congratulatory model manager.

Mandarins and management

With the largely unsuccessful attempt by George Wells to assert the primacy of the contract to settle disputes and the failure of the campaign to instil the hoped-for spirit of self-sacrifice and cooperation, other means were needed to resolve conflicts within the project. The vacuum was to be filled in part by the intervention of the government.

However, with many of the important divisions revolving around the differing interests of the German and Chinese sides, the government was hardly in a position to put itself forward as an honest broker in mediating such disputes. The local government dominated the local construction industry, both in terms of its role as a leading customer and as the principal or sole shareholder of the major construction companies. At the level of the project, the local Land Development Corporation, despite its appearance as an independent corporation, was to prove in operation little more than a department of the special zone government. The special zone itself was subordinated to the municipal government, which itself owned the general contractor and most of the subcontractors working on the project. Those it did not, such as Gang Tie, were nonetheless in part dependent on the continuing goodwill of the city government for the smooth conduct of business.

To begin with, the part played by local government officials in the running of the project took place largely behind the scenes. It was, however, to become more open as the project progressed, starting from the regular weekly meetings attended by key project officials and the special zone deputy governor, together with somewhat less frequent appearances of the special zone governor and the deputy mayor. Such close involvement is typical of major construction projects commissioned by the local government. Direct and unfettered control by officials is the norm, and that such control should have been initially somewhat muted in the case of the exhibition centre doubtless owed much to the presence of the German partner. An indication of the pattern with which both local officials and local contractors are more familiar can be gained by looking at a neighbouring project, the construction of the Science City.

The Science City is a complex of museums and educational facilities related to science and technology commissioned by the local government. As with the exhibition centre, the Science City was also accorded key project status, although in this case the municipal authority was the sole owner. The owner from the beginning of the project exercised direct and close control. Although the project was registered with the bidding office, which is supposed to ensure impartiality in assessing bids, this was generally understood to be largely a matter of form. As with all the other key projects in the city, the general contractor was part of the CCG family of companies. The project was presided over by three deputy mayors at weekly meetings at which contractors were regularly shouted at and threatened with dismissal in the event of failure to comply with instructions.

That this was no empty threat was shown by the fate of one subcontractor that found itself summarily dismissed from the project. At meetings I was able to attend, the contractors appeared completely cowed by this approach and would sit with heads bowed, not daring to answer back.

The loss threatening the contractors should they be thrown off the Science City project was not so much in terms of lost revenue, as most did not expect to make much profit from the project. Successful participation in a key project is, however, a valuable asset for career advancement and securing future contracts, despite the difficulties. In the case of the Science City, these included the shortening of the deadline by two months so that it would be completed in time for a visit President Jiang was planning to make to the area. This was decided without consultation with the contractors. While the Chinese contractors had no option but to agree, a small number of foreign contractors demurred, arguing that the change was not allowed for in the contract. As with the exhibition centre, the deadline became the principal focus of attention, leading to problems in maintaining quality.

The last point illustrates that the absence of overt conflict is not always a good sign. The Science City site may have had fewer quarrels, but this was at the expense of suppressing disagreements rather than providing any attempt to resolve them. Those who should have been advancing the cause of quality and safety were given every incentive not to do so. At least in the case of the exhibition centre the presence of the German partner and its representatives allowed greater voice to such concerns. Even though such interventions had far less effect than was hoped for, they nevertheless did have some impact. Thus the contractors did show more attention to reviewing progress against undertakings entered into at meetings under the insistence of George Wells, albeit more so on issues that did not conflict greatly with their own interests in terms of time and money. Ma Bo similarly paid more attention to pressing the contractors on quality issues following Wells' constant highlighting of the issue.

For the German partner, much difficulty was caused by the various commercial enterprises concerned, including the joint venture itself, not enjoying the degree of autonomy that they expected from the operation of enterprises bearing a similar form in Germany. The very fact that the three German exhibition centre companies all had local authorities as major shareholders may well have heightened rather than reduced the level of misunderstanding. For the three German exhibition centre companies enjoyed far more commercial autonomy than was the case with the local government companies with which they were dealing. As suggested earlier, their partner in the joint venture, the Land Development Corporation, despite having the form of an independent corporation, proved little more than a department of the local government, subject to the direct control of local civic leaders. Consequently Du, the chairman of the joint venture board, had, as a *chu* (bureau) level cadre, to seek permission from the local authority before he could travel to Germany on company business. Invited by German Fair to look at the Weserstein High-Tech Fair, for example, Du was refused permission to attend, the deputy mayor considering his presence in the city necessary given the tight construction schedule.

It would not be right, however, to portray the Chinese side as a monolithic entity. The different branches and levels of the hierarchy to which they belonged complicated coordination between the various state units. There were also problems brought about by the at times contrary pulls of hierarchical authority and commercial considerations. The interplay of these forces can be seen at work in an incident concerning City Modern Architectural Design (CMAD), the design institute working on the exhibition centre.

The design institute

CMAD's position within the state hierarchy meant that it felt able at times to ignore instructions from the special zone governor. As a municipal unit its members clearly considered it to be on equal footing with the special zone, itself under the authority of the municipality. For example, at a meeting in November, the special zone governor ordered CMAD to be at the site every day, rather than once a week as required by the contract. This contractual undertaking the governor either did not know about or chose to ignore. The CMAD representative, for his part, neither objected nor agreed, merely smiled. The instruction, however, was not carried out.

The situation was different with orders from the deputy mayor. Toward the end of November, the deputy mayor called a meeting of the joint venture, the project manager and others involved in the construction at just two hours' notice. At this meeting, he issued instructions to CMAD to assume responsibility for approving the shop drawings. This was intended to save delays resulting from obtaining approval direct from the architect. Few, however, were happy with the arrangement. CMAD itself was reluctant, as, despite its role, it had failed to familiarize itself with the project in depth. Secure in the knowledge that its involvement was required by Chinese regulations, CMAD had tended to play a largely passive role. It was accused of neglecting on a number of occasions to inform the architect of areas in which the plans came into conflict with Chinese codes, despite this being a principal reason behind the policy requiring participation of a local design institute.

The commercial department of the joint venture was also troubled by how to translate the mayor's administrative order into contractual terms. Unresolved was the issue of what should be left to the approval of the architect and what should be taken over by the design institute. Nor was there any idea as to who would bear the cost of CMAD's greater involvement. None of these complications was addressed by the deputy mayor and nobody dared to draw his attention to them at the meeting.

While CMAD was more attentive to the wishes of the deputy mayor than to the special zone governor, it should not be assumed that this was just a matter of refusing in one case and complying in the other. The mayor might not be refused, but the extent of compliance was still an open question. Although CMAD increased its presence on site, it refused to go further than facilitating communication between the contractors and the architect. CMAD refused to approve shop drawings, fearing this would bring it into conflict with the architect and breach the terms of its contract.

CMAD, as with the contractors, tended to follow the policy of nodding agreement with instructions they disagreed with, followed by delay and evasion. CMAD tended, indeed, to be somewhat more willing to risk resistance than the contractors. This was in part based on the professional status of its members. Despite the lingering echo of a respect for the heroic worker in the rhetoric of the regime, the local administrators hold the same disdain for those closely associated with manual labour as their mandarin forebears. In a society dominated for centuries by an educated elite, the professionals of the design institute were held in greater respect than the managers of the construction companies. It was an assessment in which those in the construction companies shared, frequently citing their occupation as evidence of having been born with a 'bad fate'.

A matter of taste

With the failure of the contractually instituted authority structure, the local administrators were drawn into decisions of ever more detail. The special zone deputy governor at his weekly meetings came to take on the role of a magistrate. All the trades would complain about the lack of cooperation from the other trades. The deputy governor was then expected to judge who was right and who was wrong, and who should mend their ways. At first decisions were mainly of a commercial nature, but as work progressed the local officials became more and more drawn into issues of contention involving quality considerations and matters of taste. This even reached the point where much time and attention of the deputy governor came to be taken up with the appearance of a wall.

The wall in question was to have a pure water concrete effect that was intended to display the natural qualities of the material to their fullest advantage without additional adornment. In the design intention statement the architect had stressed that one of the most important elements of the design of the building was to push conventional materials to their limits and to display good craftsmanship. This spirit was intended to guide the entire construction, leaving the design itself quite brief on specifics. However, this fundamental requirement concerning quality was unknown to many people on the project, even among those involved in the project management. Even if it had been known, however, differing aesthetic standards across the cultural divide would have made realization of the architect's dream a difficulty. Even the representative of the Chinese design institute found the notion of a bare concrete wall incomprehensible. Any discerning owner, she thought, would panel the wall and her institute would certainly not put up with a bare concrete wall prominently on display in its own office building.

Therefore, it was not surprising that the workers, failing to comprehend the architect's intention, did not pay much attention to the construction of the wall, which as a result ended up full of patches and looking generally shabby. The Jianli ordered, as was its right under the contract, that the work be redressed to improve its appearance. The contractor, unaware of the architect's intention, considered the Jianli was simply being awkward and refused. This went on for a month until the problem made its way before the special zone deputy governor for resolution. The deputy governor ordered the contractor to redress the work, but while lip-service was paid to the instruction, nothing was done. The order was repeated at a later meeting. Still nothing was done. The deputy governor, running out of patience, said that he would go to have a look at the wall for himself. Having seen it, he decided that the best thing to do was for it to be painted over. Still nothing was done. Cornering the contractor, the deputy governor was eventually able to establish that the further delay was due to having no one to pay for the paint. As usual in such circumstances, the official told the contractor to not worry about payment, but to get the work done. Still only lip-service was forthcoming. Eventually the deputy governor decided that the contractor did not need to pay for the paint, and that if the German partner would not agree to pay for it, then the Land Development Corporation should shoulder the cost. The contractor immediately bought the paint and the pure water concrete wall disappeared from sight.

The wall was not an isolated incident. The deputy governor found himself repeatedly faced with the task of resolving problems of a relatively minor nature at his regular meetings on the site. At one time or another, he was called upon to settle disputes over where materials were to be stored, how to stop workers welding in the rain, and even how to tackle workers smoking on site. Having to involve the deputy governor in such matters was widely considered by all concerned to be unsatisfactory. It was felt to be, as one leading manager from CCG remarked, 'killing mosquitoes with a cannon.' The deputy governor himself at times expressed bafflement as to why he had to deal with such matters. Despite dissatisfaction all round with this situation, it continued nonetheless. At one point, the general contractor pleaded with the deputy governor to give up the Saturday meetings, so that both he and the contractors would be spared the trouble of attendance. Gloomily the deputy governor replied this was not possible, given that he had been ordered to hold such meetings by the special zone governor. In the opinion of Dr Yu, the author of the mosquito remark:

For its part the government can't resist putting its foot in. This has been from the beginning a government contract. Everybody realizes this and so if there is any problem, they expect the government to solve it. If the government left business to business, we would not trouble them like this.

Having government officials participating so closely in the running of the project was widely felt among the managers of the contractors to retard their professional development, making them less willing and less experienced at solving problems among themselves. Whether they would have effectively assumed such responsibilities is, however, questionable, given their poor record from the early stages of the project when government officials were less in evidence. This suggested that endless squabbling over clashes of commercial interest given the absence of any effective method of dispute resolution would have been more likely than any spontaneous emergence of give-and-take.

Fractures

In June, a further serious problem emerged, one that was to worry all concerned on the project, increasing the tension over the relative weight to be accorded speed and quality still further. One of the anchor bolts securing the base of the building was found to be fractured. If this fault was shared with others, there was a serious risk that the building might collapse. However, with all the bolts imbedded in two metres of concrete, establishing whether the fault was general posed a considerable problem.

On hearing of the difficulty the structural consultant to the architect and the Moreland management team demanded that work cease and that reinforcement be provided for the pillars secured by the anchor bolts until their safety had been established. Suspending operations while this took place would mean, however, that the deadline would stand no chance of being met. The general contractor was not prepared to contemplate this. The Chinese project management team and the Chinese partner to the joint venture were equally opposed. For all, failing to meet the target or even, as the German partner and Moreland repeatedly urged, asking for the date to be put back, were unacceptable. All concerned thought it would be damaging to their careers, an open admission of failure made all the more noticeable by the tradition that key projects are invariably completed on target. The result, however, is that key projects are generally rapidly in need of renovation to correct for leaks and other faults arising from quality being sacrificed for speed.

In the case of the anchor bolts, however, the matter was understood to be more serious. To be associated with a building that collapsed would naturally be fatal to the career of those responsible and might have even more serious consequences. As the American architect put it, attempting to introduce a sense of urgency into a meeting considering what was to be done: 'Quite simply, we could all end up in gaol.'

The threat was perhaps exaggerated in its scope, but it was real enough to those likely to be held directly accountable. While the Chinese side were not prepared to cease construction and to reinforce the columns before disinterring every anchor bolt for examination, as the architect demanded, the general contractor knew that something would have to be done. It suggested that the bolts be tested where they lay, using ultrasound equipment. Gutheim, the German structural engineer acting for the architect, expressed his view that such a method was not capable of detecting fractures similar to the one already encountered if buried at depth. Privately, leading figures from the general contractor were prepared to admit this to be so. Nevertheless, the ultrasound testing went ahead. As one member of the general contractor team remarked:

> I have discussed this with the Jianli. We both agree we need to defend ourselves. In the case of the place falling down, we can always say that we have used the most advanced technology available to test to make sure. We will have done our best, and then there will not be any trouble.

In the meantime, Gutheim's instructions that work be suspended were ignored, despite it being within his contractual rights to issue such an instruction. The contractors pressed ahead and the Chinese partner refused to condone any halt to the work. The deputy general manager announced at a meeting that the joint venture had no power to command that construction stop, the project was a 'government project, and only the government has the right to call it to a halt.' The German side, for its part, sent off the broken bolt for analysis in Germany, together with other anchor bolts believed to be part of the same batch as those used. There was some doubt as to whether this was indeed true, but the Germans felt that they, too, had to do the best they could in a situation not of their own choosing. The authority structure erected by means of the contract had never been strong and by this stage was proving altogether ineffective, leaving the foreign participants frustrated and dejected as familiar levers failed to respond to their touch in matters of potentially grave importance.

A political task

As pointed out earlier, relying on the government to settle the disputes besetting the joint venture inevitably ran up against the dilemma that the local government was at one and the same time both referee and player. In certain respects, this was an advantage for the German side of the venture, for they could rely on inside assistance in overcoming regulatory obstacles. In a regulatory environment replete with uncoordinated regulatory agencies, this was undoubtedly an advantage. While official involvement smoothed conflicts in one area, however, it opened up other sources of conflict elsewhere. The intrusion of political concerns meant that more than simply the commercial health and viability of the exhibition centre was at stake as far as the Chinese partner was concerned. On the Chinese side of the project, both the Chinese partner in the joint venture and the contractors were concerned to meet the political goals of their masters in addition to meeting commercial targets.

As was illustrated in the case of the design institute, the Chinese state apparatus, however, is not a monolithic entity whose constituent elements are intent on nothing but carrying out instructions handed down from on high. Different groups and organizations within it have interests that at times cohere and at other times diverge. As reform of the state sector has progressed, commercial considerations have loomed ever larger in the minds of managers of state enterprises. On the one hand, they are concerned to enhance the bonuses funded from profits that form a substantial part of their salary. Reinforcing this concern, on the other hand, comes a new and growing concern over job security.

For much of the period of the reforms, managers continued to enjoy a privileged position in terms of job security, enjoying a status as cadres in the state apparatus established during the era of the command economy. With this came security of tenure, with transfer rather than dismissal the worst that was to be feared. Even when workers eventually began to be laid off from loss-making state units as the reforms bit deeper, the threat of redundancy did not climb high. Even this, however, is now changing and whole units have been closed, with both managers and workers facing redundancy.

The recent history of the main contractor, CCG, illustrates the situation. As mentioned earlier, CCG is in part a holding company covering all the construction companies under the public ownership of the municipality. As the reforms progressed a number of the less efficient ones were wound up and their workers laid off. Their managers, however, were transferred to other firms within the group. Shortly before construction began on the project, however, an entire unit within CCG had been closed and all staff, workers and managers included, laid off permanently. Gossip about colleagues who had met this fate was common on the site, fuelling the anxieties of CCG managers over the commercial health of their firm.

The growing importance of such commercial considerations has made units reluctant to jump to obey administrative orders when these were likely to entail substantial costs that may not be recovered. Given the power of higher municipal authorities over the careers of managers, direct refusal is seldom in evidence. Reluctance nevertheless finds expression in various attempts at evasion. Where manager and mandarin were situated on roughly the same level in terms of the state hierarchy, as in the case of the deputy special zone governor and the head of CCG, a municipal level company, complaints at costs incurred by the decisions of the deputy governor were voiced. However, Shi, one of the top leaders of CCG, would reserve expression of his complaints to personal exchanges with the deputy governor after meetings rather than voicing them more openly. At such tête-à-têtes the deputy governor would attempt to mollify the general manager, addressing him by the familiar form as '*Lao Shi* – Old Shi' and trying to reconcile him to shouldering the burden placed on his company.

Officials at meetings with the contractors would routinely tell them not to worry about matters of finance, that these would be taken care of later. Managers among themselves often expressed scepticism as to how reliable these general undertakings would prove to be. This was especially true of managers less directly related through the state hierarchy to those issuing the reassurances. Thus managers of CCG, the municipal construction company, complained frequently about delays in receiving payment from the local government, but nevertheless felt that municipal contracts could always, in the end, be relied upon to pay. Gang Tie, however, while a consortium of state-owned companies, was not a municipal company. As such, its managers had greater reason to suspect vague promises from municipal leaders that financial matters would be put right at some future date. Gang Tie was, as its managers would bemoan in such circumstances, '*bu shi qin sheng erzi* – not a child of the local authority'.

One phrase constantly made its presence felt in the conflicts between commercial and political considerations that pressed upon the Chinese participants in the project. Officials would frequently seek to put an end to objections raised concerning costs by stating that the matter was '*zhengzhi renwu* – a political task'. This phrase draws much of its force from the recent history of China. During the height of the command economy there was, indeed, little that was not a political task or could not be claimed as such. With the state plan and officials rather than the market dictating the work of organizations and individuals, people were encouraged to view their work as being a political task. The political campaigns that pervaded the period sought to boost production by stoking up ideological fervour and demonizing those thought to stand in the way of the established order. The campaigns have gone or been transformed into more harmless ritual of the type described earlier. Nevertheless, talk of political tasks still invokes uneasy memories likely to urge caution. In the context of the project this was all the more so because of the power exercised by local political officials over the Chinese joint venture partner and the state-owned construction companies. Managers in both knew they had to find a way to reconcile as best they could the economic interests of their companies with the political aspirations of their masters.

This meant that officials such as the municipal key project officer or the special zone deputy governor would frequently seek to foreclose discussion over how proposals for pushing forward with construction were to be financed with statements such as: 'This is a political task. Don't mention

money. Just do it.' Invoking the language of the political task would generally serve to bring discussion to an abrupt end. While it might stifle
opposition at the meeting table, however, it did not resolve the matter.
Once such a meeting was over, managers from contractors would gather
bitterly to voice to one another their resentment at being given tasks without
the resources to finance them. Officials would be criticized as failing to
pay any attention to how business should be done, simply attempting to
settle everything by fiat, by, as the managers used to say deprecatingly,
'*wu sha mao* – the black silk hat', a reference to the mandarin's traditional
mark of rank.

Finding themselves squeezed between a political rock and the hard place
of profit was, however, an enduring fact of life for the contractors. Once
they found themselves caught up in the logic of the political task they
knew that, much as it might hurt, it was safer to lose money than to stand
against it. For those involved in the project, the need to meet the deadline
set by the authorities entailed additional hardships. It meant working
over weekends for month after month. The lack of time this left for family
life was a source of worry. As one manager grimaced, 'I just see my wife
long enough to hand over my credit card then I'm out the door again.'
The reward for the 'model manager's wife' that featured in the campaign
reflected a widespread awareness of the strain marriages could be placed
under by the pressures borne by the managers. As with other difficulties
associated with the job, managers tend to approach this with resignation.
Asked to explain the political and economic cross pressures under which
he found himself, the leading CCG manager on the project was gloomily
fatalistic, stating in all seriousness: 'Bad fate. I must have been born with
a bad fate.'

The pressure to subordinate cost considerations to sustaining a politically
attractive image is well illustrated in arrangements for work during the
Chinese New Year in 2001. Wu Hai, head of CCG on the site, was insistent that work should continue over the holiday period so that municipal
officials could be invited on New Year's Day to congratulate the workers
on their patriotic dedication. Such visits are a regular event, the state-run
media ensuring coverage during a period noted for its high viewing figures.
Being portrayed as warm-hearted officials spending their holiday visiting
loyal workers is naturally welcomed by local politicians and providing
the opportunity of pleasing their municipal masters naturally appealed to
CCG. Gang Tie, however, being not under the direct authority of the
municipality, took a more hard-headed view of the exercise. They and their
workers, the managers insisted, would not be coming in over the holiday.
Defending their position they argued what everybody accepted, including
CCG, that the productivity of workers working over the holiday was notoriously low and would not serve to hasten the schedule. Therefore, come
New Year's Day, there were only CCG workers and managers on the site
to display to the mayor how production was being pushed forward. What

production that was taking place, however, came to a complete halt on his arrival as workers lined up to shake his hand under the gaze of the cameras. After he had driven away and the reporters had left, the site soon emptied as everybody went home early.

The political concerns of local officials were, however, something of a double-edged sword. The local government was not entirely oblivious to incurring costs; it had its own budgetary constraints. These frequently resulted in tardiness in meeting requests for payment for work undertaken by state enterprises both within and beyond their jurisdiction, contributing to the circle of debt that has long bedevilled the Chinese state sector. Knowing when and how to press for payment becomes, in such circumstances, something of an art. It is an art in which Gang Tie showed itself a consummate player in the lead up to the following New Year's Festival in 2002.

Gang Tie had remained unpaid for much of its work on the exhibition centre. There was nothing new in this. Debt arising from delay in paying for goods and services is endemic throughout the state sector, in the case of both companies and government departments. This is embedded in a number of features of the system, but one is a general sentiment that, at the end of the day, everything concerned belongs to the state. As one manager of Gang Tie who had spent time in the UK on secondment to what was then British Steel remarked: 'The situation here is totally different. Here we belong to the state and must do what the state says. It is all just a matter of Premier Zhu Rongji moving money from one of his pockets to another.'

Such an attitude leads to little sense of urgency in adjusting accounts on the part of the government. Payment is routinely delayed and the government accumulates a backlog of unpaid debts. There are circumstances, however, in which it is easier to get the authorities to loosen the purse strings. For while the political concerns of the local authorities impose burdens on the state-owned contractors, they can also at times offer the contractors a weapon. With the approach of the 2002 Chinese New Year, Gang Tie made full use of it.

In a long letter to the district governor Gang Tie outlined its achievements in constructing the exhibition halls and how it had throughout committed itself wholeheartedly to following the government's directives, including those on contributing to the maintenance of social stability. Unfortunately, the letter continues, it had still not received payment for the work it had done and had no money left to pay the migrant workers. Without resources, it could not answer for how they might react.

Hints here were all that was needed. The migrant construction workers on the site, as on many others, were paid a small basic wage for much of the year, with most withheld, to be paid in a lump sum before they return home for the annual holiday at the time of Spring Festival. To contemplate telling them they would be going home empty handed might well spark angry disturbances in the streets that the authorities are anxious to avoid. From the local politicians' point of view, leaving the migrant workers unpaid at such a time was out of the question. With the German partner refusing to agree payment before satisfactory rectification work had been completed, the district government found itself forced, belatedly, to pay seventy million yuan owed to the local development corporation, the parent of the Chinese arm of the joint venture partnership, by diverting funds allocated to another project. The development corporation was at the same time ordered to loan the general contractor fifty million yuan in order that workers on the site might be paid before the holiday.

Gang Tie's managers were clearly well pleased with the success of their ploy when I spoke to them about it. Yet, their success was not merely in playing off the commercial interests of the contractors against the political anxieties of their masters. It was, rather, due to a coalescence of forces, political, economic and traditional. While Gang Tie could play upon the anxieties of the local leaders with regard to the maintenance of public order, as managers in a state-owned enterprise their own career prospects would have been blighted had their workers actually taken to the streets.

In addition, if the workers had protested, their cause may well have elicited widespread sympathy at this time of the year. There is a traditional belief in China that one should make every effort to discharge one's debts before the old year is out. Added to this, the government still attempts to assume the mantle traditional to the ideal mandarin, the *fumuguan*, the benevolent official who is 'father and mother' to those under his care. To leave the workers to return home empty handed at the major family festivity of the year would have, on the contrary, left them looking the Chinese equivalent of Scrooge.

The single-minded concern of the German partner for the commercial success of the project in contrast to the broader concerns of the Chinese side went back to the very foundation of the joint enterprise. Recalling the initial negotiations, one of the German directors, Meyers, spoke of how he had read beforehand of the value set by the Chinese on harmony and compromise. As for the negotiations, however, he had found that on matters of fundamental interest, the Chinese seemed much the same as other people in their unwillingness to budge. Nevertheless, on other issues, the Chinese did appear to him, as the literature had led him to expect, to have a more compromising disposition. Speaking later to a Chinese participant in these negotiations, however, it emerged that it was no age-old cultural value set on harmony at work here. As she remarked: 'It had been made plain to us that the project was a political task that must go ahead. We had no alternative but to compromise.' Current institutional arrangements in China rather than purely traditional value preferences appear to have constrained the Chinese negotiators. This interpretation would appear to fit with another observation made by Meyers, for while he found his Chinese counterparts at the negotiation ready to compromise, he did not find them afraid to disturb the harmonious atmosphere of meetings by angry outbursts. Such a response does not chime well with any universal value placed on the preservation of harmony for its own sake, though it is perhaps understandable given the constraints under which the Chinese team was labouring.

From the Chinese perspective, it should not be thought that there was undiluted admiration for the commercial focus of the German partners to the joint venture. Instincts that are dictated by the market realities in which their German business partners are grounded tended at times to be elevated to the level of national characteristics and scorned as a certain narrowness by some government officials. At a visit to the project by the deputy special zone governor and head of the municipal planning bureau, the importance of pressing ahead with the second phase of the exhibition centre was raised. The officials stressed that this was necessary if the city was to hold its own in competition with other cities that were expanding their capacity in this area. The deputy general manager explained that the German side of the joint venture were very cautious at investing further, preferring to first test the market with the first phase. For the officials this seemed not a virtue, but a national vice. Reflecting on China's decision to build the world's first magnetic railway, the deputy governor remarked scornfully: 'They invented the technology for the magnetic train. However, they will not build it in their own country because they are not sure whether it will make money or not.'*

---

* Regarding such attitudes, the subsequent history of the magnetic railway is instructive. Intended to link airport and city centre, mounting costs and technical difficulties resulted in only part of the track being laid. It now terminates far out on the fringe of the city, of little practical use.

Part III

8   Conclusion

As my year of fieldwork drew towards its end, construction was still in full swing. Indeed, with little more than a month to go before the September deadline, it was intensifying, with an ever-increasing number of workers drafted onto the site. Work was going on round the clock, with stages in the construction schedule increasingly overlapping. The hanging of the glass curtain wall, the roofing, preparation of the interior and the installation of mechanical devices were all proceeding at once, increasing safety risks and fraying tempers as contractors got in each other's way. Despite these efforts, whether the centre would be ready in time for the first exhibition remained in doubt.

Yet when I returned on a follow-up visit in November, phase one was complete, the four halls were built, and an exhibition in progress. This success, however, had been costly in two ways, the first material and the second human. As for the material costs, the practice of sacrificing quality in favour of speed and cost-cutting using poor quality components was to haunt the project from its very opening. Water leaked through the ceiling and it leaked through the walls. The toilets would not flush.

Allocating responsibility for the last fault was contentious. One explanation was that the fault lay in the design, the Western architect had simply not envisaged the huge numbers who could be mobilized to descend on the exhibition centre all at once in works outings and other sponsored groups. This was dismissed by the architect, but was popular among the contractors and even the project management as shifting the blame away from their management of the construction work. Nobody was eager to recall what had been announced at a meeting of the general contractor many months earlier; that errors in marking the elevation had resulted in the building being constructed at a lower level than called for in the design. One risk, seen by some at the time but kept quiet, was that the drainage facilities would not be at the right level in relation to those of the municipality.

Quality was not the only thing to have suffered. Contrary to what might be expected, the construction managers were not exuberant at having completed the work on time. Rather the prevailing atmosphere among managers from the Chinese contractors was one of demoralization, confusion and resentment. The source of their malaise, and one of which they were clearly conscious, was the contradictory demands under which they found themselves operating. On the one hand, they were being told to run their companies as independent commercial entities, to be market oriented and to be ruled by contractual undertakings. On the other hand, they found themselves subject to being set political tasks, tasks at times issued with scant attention to the contract and with vague assurances that questions of additional costs would be attended to later. To speak of them suffering the pains of transition as China moves from a command to a market economy does not quite capture their own view of their plight. For transition implies movement, whereas what they felt was hopelessness at being mired in between both systems with little prospect of escape. Both the Land Development Corporation and CCG, the general contractor, were incorporated as independent profit-making limited-liability companies and listed on the local Stock Exchange. Yet their operation remained in practice subject to the direct and unpredictable intervention of government officials. As Pei, one of Gang Tie's managers complained:

> formerly we had one master, now we have two. The trouble is they often contradict each other. Even more confusingly, the communist master tells us to follow the market master. But then the communist master wants to drag us back and will not let us.

Such comments were often accompanied by wistful questions along the lines of 'in the West things aren't like this, are they?' Sprung, the German technical adviser, was often referred to by way of contrast, being admired and envied for having a clear and unambiguous goal.

In addition to these worries, the managers all looked haggard simply from the long hours they had been forced to work. In one instance, where the newly installed telecommunications system was failing to function properly, it had proved impossible to allocate responsibility for the fault to any one of the three firms involved. As a result, managers from all three firms were ordered to not go back home until the problem was fixed. Each was responsible for a different leg of the system and some managers doubtless felt aggrieved at being caught up in this collective punishment through no fault of their own. One manager, a German from the only foreign firm of the three, threatened to take the matter to the labour relations bureau as in breach of China's labour law, but was soon dissuaded on the grounds that he would stand little chance of success and also put his position at risk.

Decoupling

The case of the three telecommunications firms touches on a principle governing efficient organizational design, one closely related to the problems that troubled the construction of the exhibition centre. The principle states simply that if two activities are closely coupled to one another, when they are interdependent, then authority and responsibility for the two should be concentrated in the same person, body or decision-making procedure. Conversely, if one wants to allocate activities to two different firms, one needs to decouple the activities (Stinchcombe and Heimer 1985: 70). Having the activities done in sequence can help here if it is possible to clearly assess and correct any problems before the next stage commences. However, the greater the hurry, the more difficult this becomes. Let me illustrate from the site.

Occasions when work on a certain part of the building moved from one contractor to another were frequently times of increased conflict. Most commonly, this would involve the new contractor resisting taking over work that had not been completed accurately enough, causing difficulties for work on the next stage. This happened, for example, in the case of the glass curtain walls, which were to be hung by one contractor from crossbars stretched between mullions erected by another. These mullions, as mentioned earlier, were distorted, incurring extra cost and difficulty for the incoming contractor. The new contractor was a consortium that included a private firm whose managing director, under greater pressure from commercial considerations, put up fiercer resistance to proceeding under these circumstances than was characteristic of the state-owned contractors. Given that the responsibility for the deviation to the mullions had never been successfully settled, this threatened to delay the project indefinitely. Nonetheless, even this firm was eventually forced to bow under the pressure of the deadline to take over the work and proceed as best it could, feeling the weight of incurring the displeasure of the local government, given the patronage and regulatory power at its command.

The decoupling principle suggests that many of the problems at the exhibition construction site could have been solved by putting control into the same hands. Fortunately, developments on the site offered the opportunity to put this prescription to the test. This occurred through changes introduced with the start of the second phase of the project.

Phase two

With the erection of the first four halls nearing completion, thoughts turned to whether to proceed with phase two of the project, the construction of a fifth hall. The German side did not wish to proceed at this stage, partly because of the difficulties encountered in phase one, partly because they wished to use the first halls to test the market before committing further resources. The local government, however, was insistent that work should proceed on the next phase, as it had plans to increase the height of the new hall to enable the city to have a venue capable of hosting a prestigious international tennis match the following year. Accordingly, the Chinese wing of the joint venture, under instructions from the local government, agreed to stand guarantor for the loan. Not wishing to be excluded from having a part in the control of the new hall, the German side were mollified enough to go along with this arrangement providing that an agreed price was not exceeded and that its technical representative, Sprung, and Martin Li from Moreland held a watching brief over the new phase.

In practice, however, the German side of the joint venture was able to exercise even less control over the construction of the second phase than it had over the first. Martin Li was seldom able to be on the site due to commitments to other projects and the remaining lower-level Moreland staff, all Chinese, had by this time become absorbed into informal ties with the contractors to such an extent that their sympathies dulled the edge of their supervisory role. Being kept in the dark about any potentially embarrassing incidents further reduced Sprung's effectiveness. This was facilitated by the new phase having effectively become a Chinese project, with the general contractor taking its lead directly from the local government.

Relative to the first phase, control within the ownership over the progress of construction thus effectively shifted into the hands of one partner. At the same time, divisions among the contractors were removed as the general contractor's subsidiary took over sole control of erection, completely replacing Tie Building. Gang Tie was further sidelined when, eager to make up for some of its losses incurred in the first phase, its trading arm attempted to overcharge for the nodes. CCG took advantage of this to get permission from the local government to deal directly with the manufacturer, Kangzhou Valve, thus leaving Gang Tie with no more than the task of supplying the steel. Its rival had at last been ousted and CCG and its subsidiary CMC were left in possession of the field. Within CCG itself, its takeover of HK Building had, as reported earlier, effectively silenced any conflicts resulting from the difference in standards that had originally separated the two.

Evaluating the success of the structure thus in place for the second phase in comparison with the structure in the first phase is made difficult by a fact common to all such projects. This is simply that once the prototype has been developed, the copies that follow are inevitably easier as initial technical problems have been solved and the process mastered. To this extent phase two could be expected to proceed more smoothly under any organizational structure. After all, the nodes, once so puzzling to construct, were now a routine. Knowing that shifted anchor bolts would return to haunt meant that greater care was now taken to avoid disturbing them. This is not to say that construction was now entirely routine. Problems continued. Nonetheless, tensions over quality issues now largely subsided with the German side of the joint venture and its half of the project management no longer having an effective voice. With a continuing need to rush to meet a new deadline together with a tight budget, many on the project were privately ready to admit to me that unauthorized subcontractors and cheaper materials than those specified were being employed. This meant that quality problems remained, but under the new structure, they stood far less chance of coming to light.

In the circumstances prevailing on the site, moving in line with the decoupling principle to have the same or two closely related companies responsible for succeeding stages had its benefits, but it also had its costs. It might have speeded matters up, but it also covered up quality defects that needed to be addressed.

A somewhat similar situation occurred earlier in phase one with the installation of the roof membrane. This was being installed by a sister company of the firm that had just finished the roof structure, another offspring of the general contractor. A technical adviser from the manufacturer, an American, accompanied the roof membrane. At a meeting shortly after his arrival, he announced that a survey of the roof structure should be carried out before the membrane was laid. He wanted to make sure, he explained, because at his previous job in Singapore it was found, after installation was started, that the roof structure had deviated. As the roof membrane could not, or at least should not, be stretched to accommodate such deviation, time and money was wasted unnecessarily. An inspection would allow such a problem to be avoided here, he concluded helpfully, only to find the young manager of the membrane installation firm with which he had come to work turning on him angrily, advising the meeting: 'Do not listen to his nonsense. This morning he mentioned this to me. I am so upset that he suspects our work.'

Given such an attitude and squeezed between the two sister firms the adviser was soon pushed aside from active supervision. This left the installation firm free to handle and install the membrane as it saw fit, with speed once again likely to take priority over longer term quality considerations. Drawing the reins together into the same hands is not a remedy without unwelcome side effects in circumstances where quality issues can be hidden or responsibility evaded. The absence of open disputes is not always a good sign. The tension and quarrels between Gang Tie and the general contractor had served to bring to the owner's awareness problems that might well have been brushed under the carpet if they had occurred within the CCG family of firms.

Problems in the construction industry associated with the decoupling principle are frequently dealt with in the West by using the contract to institute an authoritative decision-making structure. The aim is to fashion a new unity, an effective organizational hierarchy, out of elements of the client organization and the contractor. In the present case, there was simply no effective support to enforce the authority of such a contract-based hierarchy. With the authority structures that the contract sought to erect thus proving incapable of providing effective direction, the government was drawn in to fill the vacuum and provide momentum. The aims and interests of the government were not, however, identical with those the German partner had sought to enshrine in the contract. Nor were the higher officials taking the decisions well placed to make them in an informed manner.

Not all the problems of the project can be blamed on a failure to adhere to the authority structure laid down in the contract. The contract itself was not perfect. Even if the contractors had been prepared to recognize the authority of the architect to the extent laid down in the contract, difficulties in the flow of communication would have remained. Partly this was due to differences in cultural expectations, partly simply to the novelty and complexity of the task. The latter needed a far greater presence of the architect on the site to resolve. As it was, communications at a distance were slow and ineffective, a situation compounded by the failure of the local design institute. This was far too passive in attempting to bring about understanding between the two sides.

Conversely, in evaluating the advantages and disadvantages of the different systems, the active participation of the local government had its advantages. Construction projects in China are frequently entangled in red tape, a problem from which the exhibition centre managed to find itself largely free from, saving on time, frustration and conflict. Nor should one hasten to condemn the wider concerns the government brought to the task. Seeking to rush the second phase in time to host the tennis match, for example, may well have been sensible in broader economic terms by raising the city's international profile.

Learning

I was interested to discover on my follow-up visits what the two sides, the Chinese and their foreign counterparts had learned from working together. They had certainly learned about each other, whether they had learned much from each other is more difficult to answer. What one was told depended partly on when one asked. During the heat of conflict negative stereotypes and national prejudices abounded, proving a useful stick with which to beat the other side, to justify what otherwise might well seem sharp practice, and to offer a welcome focus of self-congratulatory solidarity among those whose interests otherwise drove them apart.

Away from the heat of battle, however, the mood was more reflective and comment more balanced. Looking back and recalling what struck them as distinctive about their German colleagues, the Chinese managers tended to remark on their high standards in matters of quality, the importance they gave to matters of cost and profit, and the freedom they had to operate independently of government officials and political orders. These qualities would be mentioned in admiration, tempered by realism. Praise would quickly be followed by remarks along the lines of 'but of course that doesn't work here.' With this in mind, a weak point often attributed to the Germans was their inflexibility, their perceived failure to understand their Chinese colleagues and the Chinese situation and to adjust accordingly. Not that the Chinese system was regarded as exemplary: such remarks were often accompanied by others indicating considerable self-pity for the circumstance in which the Chinese managers found themselves and dislike of the authorities for the way they treated managers.

Apart from self-reports, more general comments can be made from observing what the Chinese participants appeared to learn from their foreign partners. Despite its attempts to evade the supervision of the Moreland project management, for example, one of the leading managers from the general contractor was busy towards the end of the project spiriting away for future use a collection of the entire range of project management forms that constituted a major part of the Moreland armoury. Yet, whether there would be the opportunity or incentive to employ them effectively is another matter. The opinion of the leading Moreland manager on the site was that the Chinese contractors had not and perhaps could not in the current circumstances, have learned the managerial skills that would have enabled them to adapt more flexibly to novel situations. As he remarked of the contractors:

> Reverting to the old system for managing phase two has lost them a valuable opportunity to learn and consolidate from phase one. They have mastered the technical difficulties of a certain type of design, that is true, but not management skills, such as coordination, communication and documentation. Nor have they developed any idea of the role of contract, the importance of quality, the role of market forces and how to get along with a foreign partner. What they have learned is not going to be relevant to what they will need in the future. Hall 5 is less troublesome as a mode, but would a foreign investor put faith in such a mode? Knowing all the problems of phase one, the Germans and Moreland would be wiser to insist on building on their own wherever possible.

This last point was indeed a lesson that the Germans had absorbed. Asked what they had learned from the project and working with their Chinese partners, those taking an active part in the construction would invariably mention that they would advise any foreign firm contemplating an equivalent project to avoid joint venturing wherever possible. This was not unrelated to another sad lesson they had learned through disappointment, that working together on the project had not fostered trust between the various parties involved. Their experience of the project seemed to them better characterized as one promoting the growth of suspicion. Interestingly from the perspective of the literature on high- and low-trust cultures touched on in Chapter 2, the Chinese side suffered no such disillusion, as they did not share such elevated expectations. When asked whether trust had built up on the project, the Chinese managers and staff said that trust was not to be expected. As one remarked, 'There was no trust to speak of. Everybody involved knew from the beginning that each party came to the project with different interests and that they were bound to clash. We expect cheating and dishonesty.'

Despite disappointment over the issue of trust, by the end of the project some of the German managers were developing a growing sense of sympathy for their Chinese counterparts. This was based on a better appreciation of the pressures with which their Chinese colleagues had to contend. Sprung, the German Fair technical representative on the site, is a case in point. Looking back over the project to assess what could have been done better, he concluded that it would have been best in the first place if the complications of a joint venture had been avoided, but, given its presence, the German side should have put in more manpower to assist and monitor. On the one hand the design, he felt, in many ways posed problems beyond the technical abilities of the Chinese contractors. There were some things CCG could do better if they had the time and money, but others they could not as they lacked the necessary expertise and experience. On the other hand, without close monitoring to keep up standards, corners were cut under pressure to meet the deadline. Nonetheless, he felt sympathy for his Chinese colleagues, who had to work under a system that was less accommodating to business needs than that in Germany. In particular, he was struck by the different role assumed by politicians and officials:

> In some ways government involvement in ownership in Germany introduces similar broader political concerns into operations than profit alone. Yet, here in China the interference often comes from individual officials whose whims are unpredictable. They appear to be a law unto themselves, simply ignoring contractual arrangements and involving themselves in management in a way that is inconceivable in Germany.

Sprung's feelings of sympathy for his Chinese colleagues were matched in return by the high regard in which he was held. He was widely admired for his professional integrity, his high standards, hard work and willingness to take responsibility for making decisions rather than passing them up the chain of command. He even received praise from Du, the chairman of the board, not noted for his generosity in such matters. The occasion was that of the first fair in the newly opened halls and the incident throws interesting light on the interaction of social identity, social distance and professional esteem. Sprung stayed at his post throughout the fair, despite being ill. Du was greatly impressed by this display of loyalty to the success of the project, commenting that 'Sprung is much better than the Foreigner.'

'The Foreigner' was the nickname by which the German general manager of the joint venture was universally known among the Chinese. This deliberately distancing title at first seems rather odd, as Steinhausen was fluent in Chinese and more familiar with Chinese manners. Sprung, on the other hand, spoke no Chinese. In contrast to Sprung, however, Steinhausen was considered lazy and unwilling to take decisions on his own authority, of being constantly in consultation with his superiors in Germany to seek backing. In fairness to Steinhausen, these beliefs may well have been a travesty of the truth. Nonetheless, they were widely held. To make matters more complex, Steinhausen was generally pilloried for conduct Chinese staff would often urge on one another as prudent, such as reporting to superiors to make sure of their backing before proceeding. He was also far more like his Chinese colleagues than his fellow Germans in his exaggeratedly meek and deferential bearing at meetings called by the special zone governor or the mayor. Despite this apparent greater closeness to his Chinese colleagues, at work here is a rather peculiar case of double standards in which foreigners were expected to behave as foreigners, to take advantage of their position to behave with the sort of freedom and integrity their Chinese colleagues admired but felt unable to emulate.

Nonetheless, the temptation to adjust to local norms was not always easy to resist. Even Sprung admitted that he felt in danger of losing his good habits and high standards, feeling the need to mix with other German businessmen to get support and assurance that he was right to be strict. Junior members of the Moreland team, as mentioned earlier, were drawn closer to the contractors through the establishment of an informal network that led to some softening of their insistence on standards stipulated under the contract. From their perspective, this was not thought of as acquiring bad habits, but learning how to adjust effectively to the circumstances in which the found themselves. As one, Xiao Miao, put it, when asked what he had learned from the project:

> First one has to do one's job well. This is most important. Otherwise one gets sacked. Second, it is very important to learn how to get along with others (*zuo ren*). There are so many complicated relationships, if one does not cope well, one could get sent off the project like George Wells. Third, a lot of Moreland ways of doing things don't work here. For example, Moreland normally will sack contractors if they do not obey orders. But here CCG [the general contractor] is more important, so they dare to disobey us. Formerly we used the quality station people to frighten the contractors into working better, but here CCG has a better relationship with the quality station people than us. And one has to learn to know how to survive under different bosses who do not get along with each other and who issue contradictory orders. One has to learn how to tell one boss about what the other boss ordered in a very careful way.

Another locally appointed Chinese member of the Moreland project management team, Zhang Ming, answered the same question about learning along similar lines:

> I have learned about the details of the contract. But most of the things I have learned in terms of good management skills and practices cannot be used on the site. You can manage, but nobody will listen to you.

A good seed cannot grow without good soil. This is very disappointing. For example, George Wells, he was very good for the project, but nobody paid any attention to him. If there had not been the government, maybe the project management could have exerted its power. But the situation on the site was we talked for hours, and nobody listened to us. However, when the governor farts, it works.

Quite why this was so brings us to the question of attitudes towards authority.

Disharmony in hierarchy

It may be recalled that in reviewing the literature on cross-cultural differences in attitudes toward authority, a number of value surveys were seen to convey the impression that China is a far more deferential society than many in the West. This tradition portrays China as a steeply hierarchical society, whose less powerful members expect and accept that power will be distributed unevenly. Leaders are expected to lead rather than to consult, subordinates to carry out instructions rather than to act on their own initiative. This is seen as meeting with general acceptance, with those lower down the hierarchy conditioned from childhood onwards into seeking harmony in hierarchy and security through dependence.

While a study such as the present one cannot claim to be able to test such cross-cultural claims, the close focus it provides nonetheless suggests such an image of Chinese attitudes towards authority is far too simple. The Confucian idyll they conjure up bears only a surface resemblance to the life of Chinese managers on the project in relation to political leaders. As I have described earlier, it is true that in the presence of the mayor their outward demeanour suggests extreme deference, as is its intention. Closer acquaintance with the views of the managers and their conduct safely out of sight of the mayor would soon disabuse one of the notion that such displays of deference are born of any inward esteem. The elaborate displays of respect paid to the officials are based on considerations that are more mundane and closely reflect the power officials have to harm those who annoy them. Officials as a class were not spoken well of by the managers. They were regarded, as we have seen, as unpredictable, dangerous and easily provoked into acts which, deliberately or otherwise, could make one's life a misery. Their guidance was frequently not welcome, except where it coincided with one's own interests. Where it did not, commands would be evaded or undermined where possible. For the officials were viewed as too remote to offer effective guidance. As one of the leading managers of Gang Tie put it: 'the mayors are far too high, they do not know about the reality. So they direct blindly.'

This is not to say that the managers were capable of running an effective project if left to their own devices, though this is what their complaints might lead one to expect. Simply removing the guiding hand of the authorities would not in itself allow business to be conducted effectively. Partly this is because the structure to which they had become used to working within had not encouraged the habit of taking responsibility. Quite the reverse, which is why many foreign firms in China wish to employ staff straight from school or university, fearful of the bad habits that those working for state-owned enterprises may have picked up (Stuttard 2000). As one of the contractors remarked, 'the construction companies and everyone else on the project should be able to do things without the government. Otherwise it is like chewing the food for the baby all the time, the baby will never be able to eat food on its own.'

Quite apart from the need to break old habits, however, there is the importance of instituting a framework that will demand and support change in a positive direction. If unlearning old ways and learning better ones is to take place there must be sufficient motivation. As Steinfeld (1998) has argued, the solution to the malaise facing state-owned enterprises in China is not simply to cut them loose from what is perceived as the dead hand of government in the expectation that then all will be well. Towards the end of the project, this was just the recipe offered by most of the Chinese managers: if only officials left the business in the hands of the managers rather than interfering, all would be fine.

Freeing up or clamping down

The interference of the officials had certainly at times hindered as much as it had helped. Yet, many of the managers had conveniently forgotten the deadlock in which the project had been caught before the intervention of the mayor gave it impetus. As the system stands at present, the officials constitute one of the few effective albeit flawed mechanisms for resolving the type of conflict in which the parties found themselves entangled.

Applying the underlying logic of Steinfeld's argument to the situation on the project one could argue that simply removing the officials from the scene would not have improved matters, unless they were replaced by a more efficient system of constraints bearing down on the parties. What was needed is not so much a freeing up as a clamping down. This, of course, is partly what the contract was intended, at least by the German side, to provide through instituting its own hierarchy of authority. Yet, in the absence of effective market discipline and an overarching rule of law binding on officials and contracting parties alike, this failed to prove effective.

In such circumstances, as we have seen, officials may well feel themselves drawn to intervene. Yet, intervention is often accompanied by an ability to evade responsibility. The case of Gang Tie illustrates this point. Looking for ways to secure compensation for having some of the erection work taken away from it and given to CMC, Gang Tie consulted a Hong Kong law firm on the possibility of winning an arbitration settlement. It was advised that arbitration would involve the government and that Gang Tie would not win if the government denied its interference. Gang Tie made an initial approach to the local authority asking it to admit to having issued the order for CMC to undertake the work. The special zone authority chose to deny this, claiming that it had merely been invited by the companies to help mediate and that it had not made any major decisions concerning the project. Gang Tie was forced to conclude that, as it was unlikely to win through arbitration given such a stand, its only recourse was to throw itself on the benevolence of the local government, despite not being under its authority. The company thus became drawn back into dependence on the benevolence of leaders through want of any other avenue to pursue.

Concluding remarks

The lessons of the present study for those contemplating a business venture in China will naturally depend on how closely their circumstances mirror those studied here. As we have seen, the advice of the foreign managers on the project was that joint venturing should be avoided wherever possible. However, as in the case of the exhibition centre, this is not always possible. The arrangements agreed to under China's accession to the World Trade Organization mean that access to a number of attractive areas of the economy, such as telecommunications and various financial services, requires Chinese participation (Tang and Ward 2003: 211–12). And despite their grumbling at the bruising they had received in joint venturing, a number of the parties involved in the construction of the exhibition centre went on to pursue further projects involving international alliances. Thus Martin Li, the Moreland project manager, went off to Beijing on a Moreland contract to supply project management to the Chinese government for the Olympics. Tempted by the same development, Gang Tie teamed up with the German structural engineer represented by Gutheim to bid, in spite of their quarrels during the course of the project. Evidently, the sad truth for those front-line managers bearing the brunt of the friction between the two sides was that at the boardroom level the figures add up, the potential profits outweigh the costs and difficulties.

Weighing up the advantages and disadvantages of a particular course of action will also vary according to the broader interests at stake. Foreign firms whose plans include substantial construction projects might do well to contemplate that one problem built in from the beginning of the present project was the complexity of the design and the high standards of craftsmanship and quality of components demanded. When these requirements came up against the insistence of the Chinese partner on using local firms lacking the necessary experience and expertise, problems were bound to result. Once these firms were adopted, there were not only the problems of technical expertise, but also differences in standards and national tastes to overcome.

This raises the difficult question of whether it might not have been wiser to use a simpler and less challenging design. In addition, too little consideration was probably given to the delays and misunderstandings consequent on having the architect stationed in America apart from occasional, because costly, visits to the site. Combining an architect intent on pushing conventional materials to their limits in an intricate design that called for great accuracy with local builders whose philosophy of construction is that if things do not fit one can always hack a bit off here or weld a bit on there, seems bound to end in mutual recrimination. Nonetheless, from the perspective of Chinese development, new skills were acquired. The city is rightly renowned for the futuristic skyline that has sprung up in recent years; one built on a spirit of being able to rise to any challenge.

For all the difficulties involved in the construction of the exhibition halls and for all the need for repairs that arose immediately, it was finished, the first group was completed. There is now an operating exhibition centre. While it fails to meet the high standards set by its architect, to most ordinary mortals it appears elegant and imposing. The future of the centre, as with its construction, is unlikely to avoid conflict. Tensions were already emerging between the Chinese partner who felt that government fairs should be offered concessionary rates and the German partner who was insisting on the joint venture using purely commercial pricing criteria. There is no reason to believe these tensions will give way to a complete coincidence of views in the future any more than they did in the past. Yet nor is there any reason to believe that these tensions will overwhelm the operation of the exhibition centre any more than they had stopped the construction of the halls. Quite apart from anything else, revenue was now being generated, recalling Martin Li's words at the beginning of the construction work that the quarrels then raging over spending money would soon be replaced by differences over making it.

The conflicts on the project throw into dramatic relief the broader strains within the mix of government intervention and free market institutions that goes to make up China's current economy. The government moves back and forth between the two poles, expecting firms to be governed by the market and the pursuit of profit at one moment and setting political goals for them the next. Nor can foreign firms be excused from perpetuating this. The German partners to the joint venture were not above seeking to pressure the local government into giving assurances that competitors would be excluded from the city. Nor did they hesitate to press to be excluded from the supervision of regulatory bodies intended to ensure fair trade in the matter of tendering. Such lobbying for political favours is commonplace. In a sense it is understandable, as the implementation and administration of laws and regulations in China often falls far short of their professed aim. Given such shortcomings special pleading is to be expected. Nonetheless, it contributes to a vicious circle that hinders development of the rule of law.

Prescribing the rule of law and praising the benefits of hard budgetary constraints backed up by market sanctions is one thing, bringing them about another. The whole panoply of institutions on which they rest were not arrived at overnight in the West and the particular form institutions have taken there is a product of the historical juncture at which they developed. China's own history and the circumstances it confronts both domestically and internationally will continue to ensure that whatever business system it fashions will be one with Chinese characteristics. Westerners expecting to find in China either now or in the future a system that is a replica of their own are set for a disappointment.

They would be better advised to approach the situation with an awareness that things are unlikely to be as they appear. Institutions, roles and practices bearing a surface resemblance to those familiar from home are likely to operate in quite a different fashion given the business milieu prevailing in China. Conversely, where matters are clearly different, so different as to be conducted in what appears to be an irrational manner, this should not automatically be attributed to ignorance. There are doubtless occasions where this may be the case, but often there is a method to apparent madness, a reason for certain practices that is rooted in the logic of the situation confronting those involved. Understanding this is likely to prove more effective in getting to grips with the situation than simply dismissing out of hand as the consequence of ignorance and folly all practices that fail to comply with the norms of Western business. This is perhaps easier said than done, as to the outsider the conflicting pressures to which Chinese managers are exposed are often hidden from sight. Hopefully the present study will have gone some way towards remedying this.

Appendix
Organizations and individuals mentioned in the text

Organizations

Altdurf Fair: one of the three members of German Fair, the German half of the joint venture.

Anke: the German structural engineering consultant employed by the architect.

City Construction Group (CCG): the Chinese joint venture partner of the general contractor.

City Mechanical Construction (CMC): one of two subcontractors erecting the steel structure, a subsidiary of City Construction Group.

City Modern Architectural Design (CMAD): the Chinese design institute contracted to advise the architect.

City Nuclear Power Design Institute: a shop drawing sub-subcontractor.

City Number 9 Construction Company: the civil engineering subcontractor, a subsidiary of City Construction Group.

City Number 11 Construction Company: the Chinese partner in the Korean Construction/Number 11 consortium bidding for the project, a subsidiary of City Construction Group.

City Number 13 Construction Company: the mechanical and electrical installation subcontractor, a subsidiary of City Construction Group.

City Number 15 Steel Company: owner of Metallurgical Construction, acquired recently by Gang Tie Group.

Dayu: the general Jianli, or quality supervisor employed by the owner, a *minying* subsidiary of a state-owned construction research institute.

Gang Tie Consortium: the steelwork subcontractor nominated by the owner, a consortium of Metallurgical Construction, International Trade and Tie Building.

Gang Tie Group: a Chinese iron and steel conglomerate, part owner of Gang Tie Consortium.

German Fair: the German partner of the International Exhibition Centre, a joint venture of Weserstein Fair, Altdurf Fair and Rhernseld Fair.

Glazier: the curtain wall subcontractor, a joint venture of a German company and a Chinese company.

HK Building: the Hong Kong joint venture partner of the general contractor, acquired later by City Construction Group.

International Exhibition Centre: the owner of the project, a joint venture between German Fair and the Land Development Corporation.

International Trade Company: one of the three members of the Gang Tie Consortium, a subsidiary of Gang Tie Group.

Interstall: the German roof membrane design consultant employed by the architect.

Jianli: the Chinese quality supervisor.

Jinrong Land Development Corporation: one of the two land development corporations in the city, it acquired Land Development Corporation during the project.

Kangzhou Valve: the steel node manufacturer supplying Gang Tie Consortium.

Keyi: the steelwork Jianli, or quality supervisor, a *minying* subsidiary of a state-owned steel research institute.

KIR: the German mechanical and electrical consulting company, part of the Moreland project management team.

Korean Construction: a partner of the Korean Construction/Number 11 consortium bidding for the project, the subsidiary of a Korean conglomerate.

Land Development Corporation: the Chinese joint venture partner of the International Exhibition Centre, one of the two land development corporations in the city.

Mayfair: a British conglomerate.

Metallurgical Construction: one of the three partners of the Gang Tie Consortium, in charge of manufacturing the steelwork and project management, a subsidiary of City Number 15 Steel Company.

Moreland: a British multinational project management company.

Pagoda: the steelwork fabrication sub-subcontractor, a subsidiary of Metallurgical Construction, a Hong Kong–mainland Chinese joint venture.

Rhernseld Fair: one of the three partners of German Fair, the German half of the joint venture.

Tiandi: the quantity surveyor, part of the Chinese owner's project management team.

Tie Building: one of the three members of the Gang Tie Consortium, a former subsidiary of the state Number 23 Metallurgical Construction Company, now an independent company operating in the city.

Weserstein Fair: one of the three partners of German Fair, the German half of the joint venture.

Young and Muller: the American architect based in the United States.

Individuals

Braun: a German mechanical and electrical engineer from KIR working in the Moreland project management team.

Chen: a government official from the municipal key project office.

Croce: the American architect from Young and Muller.

Du Yinhua: head of the Jinrong Land Development Corporation, later to replace Wang Ke as the chairman of the board of the International Exhibition Centre.

Gao: a senior civil engineer from the Land Development Corporation, sent to supervise technical issues on the project.

Gutheim: the German structural engineer from Anke acting on behalf of the architect as the chief structural engineer for the International Exhibition Centre.

Huang Xi: the owner of a private construction company whose migrant workers were eventually to work on the project.

Ji: a senior engineer from Pagoda acting as the chief engineer for the Gang Tie Consortium.

Lan Shoudong: a Chinese Australian from Moreland working in the technical department of the Moreland project management team.

Li Jie: a junior manager from the Land Development Corporation, acted as the campaign organizer.

Li, Martin: a Chinese Canadian civil engineer and project manager from Moreland, deputy head of the project management team.

Ma Bo: a project manager from the Land Development Corporation, head of the project management team.

Mao Yaming: a structural engineer from the Land Development Corporation, a member of the technical staff in the Chinese project management team.

Meyers: a director of Rhernseld Fair, CEO of German Fair.

Pei: a manager from International Trade, part of the Gang Tie Consortium.

Shen: a manager from Metallurgical Construction, head of the Gang Tie Consortium.

Shi: head of City Construction Group.

Sprung: a mechanical and electronic engineer from Altdurf Fair, sent by German Fair to supervise the project.

Steinhausen: the general manager of the International Exhibition Centre employed by German Fair.

Wang Ke: deputy general manager of the Land Development Corporation, chairman of the board of directors of the International Exhibition Centre, later to be replaced by Du.

Weinmuller: a senior civil engineer from Weserstein Fair, sent to supervise the project, later to be replaced by Sprung.

Wells, George: an American member of the Moreland project management team, introduced to the project in an attempt to lift quality standards.

Wu Hai: a senior manager from City Number 9 Construction Company, acting as the deputy general manager of the general contractor.

Xiao Bao: head of one of the erection teams of Tie Building.

Xiao Miao: a civil engineer, a junior member of the technical department of the Moreland project management team.

Xu: head of the International Trade, part of the Gang Tie Consortium.

Yu: chief engineer of the City Number 9 Construction Company, acting as the chief engineer of the general contractor.

Zhang Haiying: a bureaucrat from the municipal government nominated as the deputy general manager of the International Exhibition Centre.

Zhang Ming: a civil engineer, one of the junior technical staff from the Moreland project management team.

Zhao Wenyan: an interpreter from International Trade, employed by the Chinese project management team to interpret for Ma Bo.

Zhuang: a retired general manager from City Mechanical Construction, eventually one of the steel erection subcontractors.

Bibliography

Ackroyd, S. and Thompson, P. (1999) *Organizational Misbehaviour*, London: Sage.

Barley, N. (1987) *A Plague of Caterpillars*, Harmondsworth: Penguin Books.

Bodde, D. and Morris, C. (1967) *Law in Imperial China*, Cambridge, Mass.: Harvard University Press.

Bond, M.H. and Hwang, K.K. (1986) 'The social psychology of the Chinese people', in M.H. Bond (ed.) *The Psychology of the Chinese People*, Oxford: Oxford University Press.

Bond, M.H. and King, A.Y.C. (1985) 'Coping with the threat of westernisation in Hong Kong', *International Journal of Intercultural Relations*, 5: 137–52.

Bond, M.H. and Lee, P.W.H. (1981) 'Face-saving in Chinese culture', in A.Y.C. King and R.P.L. Lee (eds) *Social Life and Development in Hong Kong*, Hong Kong: Chinese University Press.

Burrell, G. and Morgan, G. (1979) *Sociological Paradigms and Organisational Analysis: Elements of the Sociology of Corporate Life*, London: Heinemann.

Child, J. (1981) 'Culture, contingency and capitalism in the cross-cultural study of organizations', *Research in Organizational Behaviour*, 3: 303–56.

Child, J. (1994) *Management in China during the Age of Reform*, Cambridge: Cambridge University Press.

Child, J. (1995) 'Follett: constructive conflict' in P. Graham (ed.) *Mary Parker Follett – Prophet of Management*, Boston, Mass.: Harvard Business School Press.

Child, J. and Markóczy, L. (1994) 'Host country managerial behaviour in Chinese and Hungarian joint ventures', in M. Boisot (ed.) *East–West Business Collaboration: the Challenge of Governance in Post-socialist Enterprises*, London: Routledge, 127–48.

Clegg, S. (1975) *Power, Rule and Domination: a Critical and Empirical Understanding of Power in Sociological Theory and Organizational Life*, London: Routledge & Kegan Paul.

Colson, E. (1975) *Tradition and Contract: the Problem of Order*, London: Heinemann.

Cooley, C.A. (1966) [1918] *Social Process*, Carbondale, Ill.: South Illinois University Press.

Dawson, S. (1996) *Analysing Organisations*, London: Macmillan.

Dore, R. (1990) *British Factory – Japanese Factory: the Origins of National Diversity in Industrial Relations*, Berkeley, Calif.: University of California Press.

Eisenhardt, K.M. (1989) 'Agency theory: an assessment and review', *Academy of Management Review*, 14, 1: 57–74.

Fukuyama, F. (2000) 'Social capital', in L.E. Harrison and S.P. Huntingtion (eds) *Culture Matters: How Values Shape Human Progress*, New York: Basic Books.

Gao, G., Ting-Toomey, S. and Gudykunst, W.B. (1996) 'Chinese communication processes', in M.H. Bond (ed.) *The Handbook of Chinese Psychology*, Hong Kong: Oxford University Press.

Goffman, E. (1961) *Asylums*, New York: Doubleday.

Goody, J. (1996) *The East in the West*, Cambridge, Mass.: Cambridge University Press.

Graham, P. (ed.) (1995) *Mary Parker Follett – Prophet of Management*, Boston, Mass.: Harvard Business School Press.

Gulliver, P.H. (1979) *Disputes and Negotiations: a Cross-cultural Perspective*, New York: Academic Press.

Guthrie, D. (1999) *Dragon in a Three-piece Suit: the Emergence of Capitalism in China*, Princeton, N.J.: Princeton University Press.

Hertz, E. (1998) *The Trading Crowd: an Ethnography of the Shanghai Stock Market*, Cambridge: Cambridge University Press.

Higgin, G. and Jessop, N. (1965) *Communications in the Building Industry*, London: Tavistock.

Hildebrandt, H.W. (1988) 'A Chinese managerial view of business communication', *Management Communication Quarterly*, 2: 217–34.

Hofstede, G. (1980) *Culture's Consequences: International Differences in Work-related Values*, Beverly Hills, Calif.: Sage.

Hofstede, G. (1994) *Cultures and Organizations*, London: HarperCollins.

Hofstede, G. and Bond, M. (1988) 'The Confucian connection: from cultural roots to economic growth', *Organizational Dynamics*, 16, 4: 4–21.

Hsiao, K.C. (1979) *Compromise in China*, Seattle: University of Washington.

Hwang, K.K. (1990) 'Modernization of the Chinese family business', *International Journal of Psychology*, 25: 593–618.

Johnston, A.I. (1995) *Cultural Realism*, Princeton, N.J.: Princeton University Press.

Leach, E. (1982) *Social Anthropology*, Oxford: Oxford University Press.

Leung, K. (1987) 'Some determinants of reactions to procedural models for conflict resolution: a cross-national study', *Journal of Personality and Social Psychology*, 53: 898–908.

Macaulay, S. (1963) 'Non-contractual relations in business', *American Sociological Review*, 28, 1: 55–67.

Mead, R. (1990) *Cross-cultural Management Communication*, Chichester: Wiley.

Mo, J.S. (1997) 'Alternative dispute resolution', in C.G. Wang and X.C. Zhang (eds) *Introduction to Chinese Law*, Hong Kong: Sweet & Maxwell.

Moser, M.J. (1995) 'Dispute settlement', in D. Lewis (ed.) *Life and Death of a Joint Venture*, London: Asia Law and Practice.

Palmer, M.J. (1991) 'Mediation in the People's Republic of China', in K.J. Mackie (ed.) *A Handbook of Dispute Resolution*, London: Routledge.

Pettigrew, A. (1973) *The Politics of Organisational Decision Making*, London: Tavistock.

Pye, L. (1982) *Chinese Commercial Negotiating Style*, Cambridge, Mass.: Oelgeschlager, Gunn and Hain.

Ralston, D.A., Gustafson, D.J., Cheung, F.M. and Terpstra, R.H. (1993) 'Differences in managerial values: a study of U.S., Hong Kong and PRC managers', *Journal of International Business Studies*, 24: 249–75.

Ralston, D.A., Egri, C.P., Stewart, S., Terpstra, R.H. and Yu, K. (1999) 'Doing business in the 21st century with the new generation of Chinese managers: a study of generational shifts in work values in China', *Journal of International Business Studies*, 30, 2: 415–28.

Ralston, D.A., Yu, K.C., Wang, X., Terpstra, R.H. and Ho, W. (1996) 'The cosmopolitan Chinese manager: findings of a study on managerial values across the six regions of China', *Journal of International Management* 2: 79–109.

Redding, S.G. (1993) *The Spirit of Chinese Capitalism*, Berlin: de Gruyter.

Redding, S.G. and Ng, M. (1983) 'The role of "face" in the organizational perceptions of Chinese managers', *International Studies of Management and Organization*, XIII, 3: 92–123.

Rowe, W. T. (1984) *Hankow: Commerce and Society in a Chinese City, 1796–1889*, Stanford, Calif.: Stanford University Press.

Roy, D. (1960) 'Banana time: job satisfaction and informal interaction', *Human Organization*, 18: 158–68.

Steinfeld, E.S. (1998) *Forging Reform in China: the Fate of State-owned Industry*, Cambridge: Cambridge University Press.

Stinchcombe, A.L. and Heimer, C.A. (1985) *Organization Theory and Project Management*, Oslo: Norwegian University Press.

Stuttard, J.B. (2000) *The New Silk Road*, New York: John Wiley.

Tang, J. and Ward, A. (2003) *The Changing Face of Chinese Management*, London: Routledge.

Tang, S.F. and Kirkbride, P.S. (1986) 'Developing conflict management skills in Hong Kong: an analysis of some cross-cultural implications', *Management Education and Development*, 17, 3: 287–301.

Thomas, K. (1992) 'Conflict and conflict management', in M.D. Dunnette and L.M. Hough (eds) *Handbook of Industrial and Organizational Psychology, Volume 3*, Pao Alto, Calif.: Consulting Psychologists Press.

Trompenaars, F. (1993) *Riding on the Waves of Culture*, London: Brealey.

Tse, D.K., Francis, J. and Walls, J. (1994) 'Cultural differences in conducting intra- and inter-cultural negotiations: a Sino-Canadian comparison', *Journal of International Business Studies*, 25: 537–55.

Walder, A.G. (1995) 'Local governments as industrial firms: an organizational analysis of China's transitional economy', *American Journal of Sociology*, 101: 263–301.

Wang, G.G. (1993) *Business Law in China*, Hong Kong: Butterworth.

Warner, M. and Ng, S.H. (1998) 'Is a collective bargaining institution in the making inside China?', Chinese Management Centre Working Paper, University of Hong Kong.

Weber, M. (1951) *The Religion of China*, Glencoe, Ill.: Free Press.

Weldon, E. and Jehn, K.A. (1996) 'Conflict management in US–Chinese joint ventures: an analytical framework', in J. Child and Y. Lu (eds) *Management Issues in China: International Enterprises*, London: Routledge.

Whitley, R.D. (1992) *Business Systems in East Asia*, London: Sage.

Williamson, O.E. (1981) 'The modern corporation: origins, evolution, attributes', *Journal of Economic Literature*, 19: 1537–68.

Wu, D.Y.H. (1996) 'Chinese childhood socialization', in M.H. Bond (ed.) *The Handbook of Chinese Psychology*, Hong Kong: Oxford University Press.

Yang, K.S. (1986) 'Chinese personality and its change', in M.H. Bond (ed.) *The Psychology of the Chinese People*, Oxford: Oxford University Press.

Yang, K.S. (1996) 'Psychological transformation of the Chinese people as a result of societal modernization', in M.H. Bond (ed.) *The Handbook of Chinese Psychology*, Hong Kong: Oxford University Press.

Yates, J.F. and Lee, J.W. (1996) 'Chinese decision-making' in M.H. Bond (ed.) *The Handbook of Chinese Psychology*, Hong Kong: Oxford University Press.

Young, L.W.L. (1982) 'Inscrutability revisited', in J.J. Gumperz (ed.) *Language and Social Identity*, Cambridge: Cambridge University Press.

Yu, X. (1995) 'Conflict in a multi-cultural organization: an ethnographic attempt to discover work-related cultural assumptions between Chinese and American co-workers', *International Journal of Conflict Management*, 6: 211–232.

Index